248

IN HIS OWN WRITE
&
A SPANIARD IN THE WORKS

'It was fun to be around John as we were feeding this comedy machine. He was funny then and the books are still great... Even our children find them just as much fun as we did.'

George Harrison

'John's inscription on my copy of *A Spaniard in the Works* when it first came out in 1965 says it all: "To Ringo with love, you dwarf bastard".'

Ringo Starr

'With one bound copy of *In His Own Write* John was free! He had made a giant leap out of the box marked "Pop Star". What a career move! Jonathan Cape offered him a golden key, allowing him into a garden not visited by peers or predecessors. His three comrades, to their undying credit, begrudged him none of it and gave him joyful support. But from then on John was "the literary Beatle" and the halo shines on to this day.'

Derek Taylor

IN HIS OWN WRITE
&
A SPANIARD IN THE WORKS

JOHN LENNON

With a new introduction by Jon Savage

PIMLICO

PIMLICO
An imprint of Random House
20 Vauxhall Bridge Road,
London SW1V 2SA

Random House Australia (Pty) Limited
20 Alfred Street, Milsons Point, Sydney
New South Wales 2061, Australia

Random House New Zealand Limited
18 Poland Road, Glenfield, Auckland 10, New Zealand

Random House South Africa (Pty) Limited
Endulini, 5A Jubilee Road, Parktown 2193, South Africa

Random House UK Ltd Reg. No. 954009

In His Own Write first published by Jonathan Cape 1964
A Spaniard in the Works first published by Jonathan Cape 1965
Pimlico edition 1997

9 10 8

Printed and bound in Great Britain
by Butler and Tanner Ltd, Frome and London

ISBN 0-7126-6615-X

Introduction to the Pimlico edition
by Jon Savage

By December 1963, it had become clear that the Beatles were more than just a pop group. They were already a national sensation – the phrase 'Beatlemania' had been coined after their 13 October appearance at the London Palladium – but instead of levelling off, the hysteria that surrounded their every move only increased over the next few months. By April 1964, when the Beatles held the top five placings in the Billboard US singles chart, they were an unprecedented phenomenon: no group from Britain, let alone Liverpool, had so totally captured the imagination of the Western world.

John Lennon's first book, *In His Own Write*, spans this period of lift off: from national to international success, from mere pop stars to serious artists, from an entertainment to a social and political event. It happened by chance. According to Tom Maschler, then Literary Director of Jonathan Cape, 'the idea stemmed from a book I had commissioned about the Beatles, by an American journalist called Michael Braun.[1] In the middle of the book, Braun handed me several little ditties: I thought they were wonderful and asked him who wrote them. When he told me John Lennon, I was immensely excited.'

Braun had been on the road with the group on their winter 1963 tour, and suggested that Maschler come down to a fan club showcase at the Wimbledon Palais on 14 December: as he reported the event in *Love Me Do*, 'the dance floor was totally pagan. They were auctioning pictures of the Beatles, and the larger ones brought deafening screams'. Maschler remembers the concert as 'delightful, joyful and charming... Afterwards I went back to meet Lennon and the other Beatles. At the back of the theatre there was a bar with a grid that came down like chain mail. The fans were going by, pushing their programmes under the chain mail for the boys to sign. One in six keeled over: I must have seen 100 people faint. It went on for at least an hour.'

'Then I began to see John at his flat in Emperor's Gate. He hadn't been writing for publication – just doodling on pieces of paper in hotel rooms. I encouraged him to produce more pieces, and also persuaded him to do more drawings. I chose the title out of a list of about 20 he had suggested. Alternatives were *The Transistor Negro*, *Left Hand Left Hand* (after Osbert Sitwell's *Left Hand Right Hand*), and *Stop One and Buy Me*. John was quick, witty, harsh. If you made a false move, he would slap you down. His perception was very acute: if things were going well, he was a delight. If you didn't see the point, he would make you feel worse. I found him very engaging.'

The contract for *In His Own Write* was signed on 6 January for an advance of £1000. Jonathan Cape got 31 pieces of writing – stories, parodies, poems, an introduction from Paul McCartney, and enough drawings to fill what would be 80 pages. Beautifully designed, and topped by an iconic Robert Freeman photograph, *In His Own Write* was a slim but timely volume. Published on 23 March 1964, it was an immediate best-seller. 'We printed 25,000 but before publication it wasn't easy to subscribe that number', says Tom Maschler. 'There was resistance; it was thought that it would be a seven-day wonder. Then on the Sunday, we got incredible reviews in virtually every newspaper, including the *Observer* and the *Sunday Times*[2]. Suddenly we had a literary bestseller.'

'On the Monday, when I came into the office, there was a queue of booksellers and reps outside the warehouse. It's the only time I've ever seen booksellers queue for anything: some had ordered one copy and were coming back for 24.' *In His Own Write* reprinted twice during the last week of March, and by January 1965 had gone through five more printings, selling nearly 200,000 copies within ten months. By the time sales were falling off, there was a second Lennon volume. Published on 24 June 1965, *A Spaniard in the Works* went through four impressions (and 100,000 sales) within three months.

When John Lennon wrote these books, the Beatles were still in the habit of singing lyrics about 'diamonds and rings'. What came out of his head was spontaneous and uncensored: 'I hardly ever alter anything', John Lennon told Wilfred De'Ath in a June 1965 *World of Books* radio interview. 'Because I'm selfish about what I write or big-headed about it. Once I've written it I like it and the publisher sometimes says, you know, shall we leave this out or change that and I fight like mad because once I've done it, I like to keep it. But I always write it straight off.' What you get is an alternative take on the Beatles' public sweetness and light: sick parodies, surreal low life tales, vengeful attacks on the media. Nobody is spared.

And these jottings stick like splinters in the mind. Quite apart from their sheer sense of fun and play – the incredible fertility of Lennon's malapropisms and neologisms: that Liverpool Irish–English subversion of the ruling-class language – they also represent a crucial phase in John Lennon's development as a writer, offering a breakthrough from the teen romance format that had become a prison for the Beatles as early as spring 1964. Here he could find an outlet for his obsession with the Goons and Lewis Carroll. 'I change words because I haven't a clue what words mean half the time', Lennon admitted in June 1965, but he initiated a new language that, as part of the Beatles' visual, aural and verbal package, was spread around the world.

In *Revolution in the Head*, Ian MacDonald claims that 'the eminent journalist, Kenneth Allsop, whom Lennon admired, challenged him as to why his songs didn't employ the acerbic wordplay of his books'. Prodded also by Bob Dylan, Lennon started to write darker, deeper songs through 1965 and 1966: 'In My Life', 'Girl', 'Norwegian Wood', 'Dr Robert', 'Rain', culminating in 1967 with what might be the greatest Beatles song, 'I am the Walrus' - where the buried anger, pin-sharp word-play and stream of consciousness aesthetic of these two books find their fullest expression. Those songs and lyrics went directly into the cerebral cortexes of millions: their continued power is illustrated by the incredible success of the Beatles' 1995/6 *Anthology* campaign: three double CD discs that have sold more than almost every single Beatles album first time around.

Here are two snapshots from 1964 and 1965, from the heart of Beatlemania: here is the man in the eye of the storm, revealing his shadow.

[1] *Love Me Do: The Beatles' Progress*, Penguin 1964, republished 1996.
[2] Sunday 22 March, the day before official publication. Sample quote, from George Melly's review in the *Sunday Times*: 'It is fascinating of course to climb inside a Beatle's head to see what's going on there, but what really counts is that what's going on there really is fascinating.'

JOHN LENNON IN HIS OWN WRITE

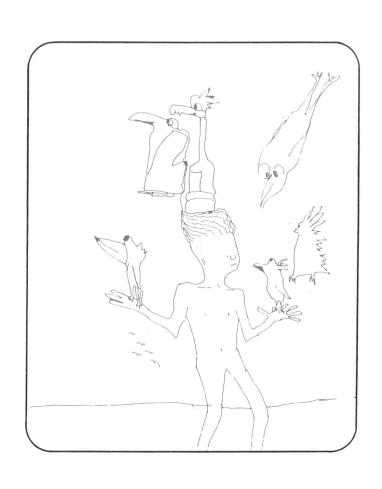

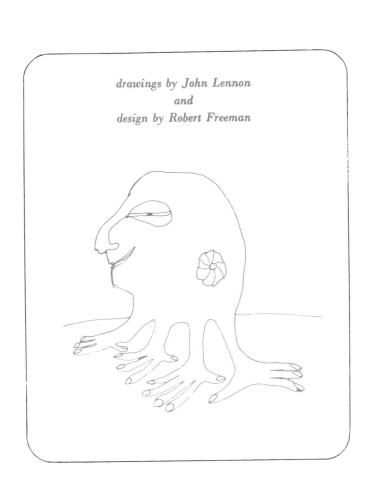

drawings by **John Lennon**
and
design by **Robert Freeman**

CONTENTS

Introduction	5
Partly Dave	9
No Flies on Frank	11
Good Dog Nigel	14
At the Denis	16
The Fat Growth on Eric Hearble	18
The Wrestling Dog	20
Randolf's Party	23
The Famous Five through Woenow Abbey	26
Sad Michael	29
I Wandered	30
A Letter	31
Scene three Act one	32
Treasure Ivan	36
All Abord Speeching	39
The Fingletoad Resort of Teddiviscious	42
Alec Speaking	44
Liddypool	48
You Might Well Arsk	49
Nicely Nicely Clive	50
Neville Club	54
The Moldy Moldy Man	55
*On Safairy with Whide Hunter	56
I Sat Belonely	58
Henry and Harry	60
Deaf Ted, Danoota, (and me)	62
A Suprise for Little Bobby	64
Halbut Returb	65
Unhappy Frank	66
On this Churly Morn	68
Victor Triumphs Again	70
and Mrs. Weatherby Learns a Lesson	
I Remember Arnold	72

* Written in conjugal with Paul.

INTRODUCTION

At Woolton village fete I met him. I was a fat school-boy and, as he leaned an arm on my shoulder, I realised that he was drunk. We were twelve then, but, in spite of his sideboards, we went on to become teenage pals.

Aunt Mimi, who had looked after him since he was so high, used to tell me how he was cleverer than he pretended, and things like that. He had written a poem for the school magazine about a hermit who said: 'as breathing is my life, to stop I dare not dare.' This made me wonder right away – 'Is he deep?' He wore glasses so it was possible, and even without them there was no holding him. 'What 'bus?' he would say to howls of appreciative laughter.

He went to Quarry Bank High School for Boys and later attended to the Liverpool Art College. He left school and played with a group called the Beatles, and, here he is with a book. Again I think – 'Is he deep?' 'Is he arty, with it or cultured?'

There are bound to be thickheads who will wonder why some of it doesn't make sense, and others who will search for hidden meanings.
'What's a Brummer?'
'There's more to 'dubb owld boot' than meets the eye.'
None of it has to make sense and if it seems funny then that's enough.

Paul

P.S. I like the drawings too.

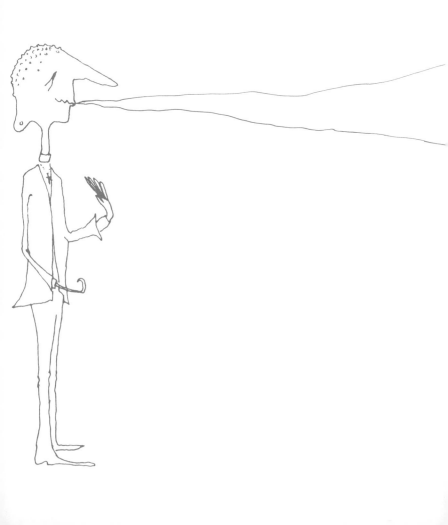

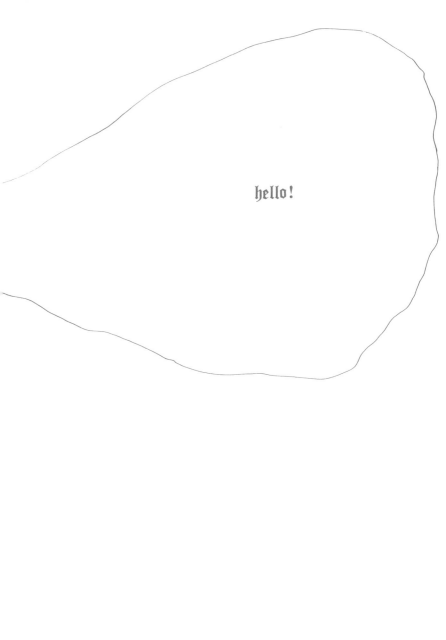

hello!

Partly Dave

There once upon a time was a man who was partly Dave – he had a mission in life. 'I'm partly Dave' he would growm in the morning which was half the battle. Over breakfast he would again say 'I am partly Dave' which always unnerved Betty. 'Your in a rut Dave' a voice would say on his way to work, which turned out to be a coloured conductor! 'It's alright for you.' Dave used to think, little realising the coloured problem.

Partly Dave was a raving salesman with the gift of the gob, which always unnerved Mary. 'I seem to have forgotten my bus fare, Cobber,' said Dave not realising it. 'Gerroff the bus then' said Basubooo in a voice that bode not boot, not realising the coloured problem himself really. 'O.K.' said partly Dave, humbly not wishing to offend. 'But would you like your daughter to marry one?' a voice seem to say as Dave lept off the bus like a burning spastic.

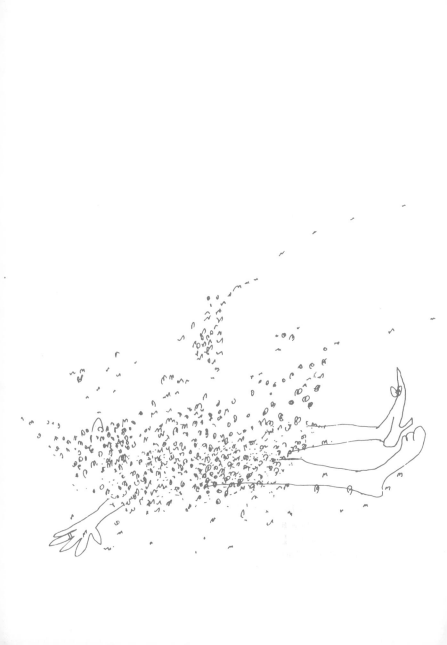

No Flies on Frank

There were no flies on Frank that morning – after all why not? He was a responsible citizen with a wife and child, wasn't he? It was a typical Frank morning and with an agility that defies description he leapt into the barthroom onto the scales. To his great harold he discovered he was twelve inches more tall heavy! He couldn't believe it and his blood raised to his head causing a mighty red colouring.

'I carn't not believe this incredible fact of truth about my very body which has not gained fat since mother begat me at childburn. Yea, though I wart through the valet of thy shadowy hut I will feed no norman. What grate qualmsy hath taken me thus into such a fatty hardbuckle.'

Again Frank looked down at the awful vision which clouded his eyes with fearful weight. 'Twelve inches more heavy, Lo!, but am I not more fatty than my brother Geoffery whose father Alec came from Kenneth – through Leslies, who begat Arthur, son of Eric, by the house of Ronald and April – keepers of James of Newcastle who ran Madeline at 2–1 by Silver Flower, (10–2) past Wot-ro-Wot at 4/3d a pound?'

He journeyed downstairs crestfallen and defective – a great wait on his boulders – not even his wife's battered face could raise a smile on poor Frank's head – who as you know had no flies on him. His wife, a former beauty queer, regarded him with a strange but burly look.

'What ails thee, Frank?', she asked stretching her prune. 'You look dejected if not informal,' she addled.

'Tis nothing but wart I have gained but twelve inches more tall heavy than at the very clock of yesterday at this time – am I not the most miserable of men? Suffer ye not to spake to me or I might thrust you a mortal injury; I must traddle this trial alone.'

'Lo! Frank – thou hast smote me harshly with such grave talk – am I to blame for this vast burton?'

Frank looked sadly at his wife – forgetting for a moment the cause of his misery. Walking slowly but slowly toward her, he took his head in his hands and with a few swift blows had clubbed her mercifully to the ground dead.

'She shouldn't see me like this,' he mubbled, 'not all fat and on her thirtysecond birthday.'

Frank had to get his own breakfast/that morning and also on the following mornings.

Two, (or was it three?) weeks later Frank awake again to find that there were *still* no flies on him.

'No flies on this Frank boy,' he thought; but to his amazement there seemed to be a lot of flies on his wife – who was still lying about the kitchen floor.

'I carn't not partake of bread and that with her lying about the place,' he thought allowed, writing as he spoke. 'I must deliver her to her home where she will be made welcome.'

He gathered her in a small sack (for she was only four foot three) and headed for her rightful home. Frank knocked on the door of his wife's mothers house. She opened the door.

'I've brought Marian home, Mrs. Sutherskill' (he could never call her Mum). He opened the sack and placed Marian on the doorstep.

'I'm not having all those flies in my home,' shouted Mrs. Sutherskill (who was very houseproud), shutting the door. 'She could have at least offered me a cup of tea,' thought Frank lifting the problem back on his boulders.

Good Dog Nigel

Arf, Arf, he goes, a merry sight,

Our little hairy friend,

Arf, Arf, upon the lampost bright

Arfing round the bend.

Nice dog! Goo boy,

Waggie tail and beg,

Clever Nigel, jump for joy

Because we're putting you to sleep at thre

of the clock, Nigel.

At the Denis

Madam: I have a hallowed tooth that suffer me grately.

Sir: Sly down in that legchair Madam and open your gorble wide – your mouse is all but toothless.

Madam: Alad! I have but eight tooth remaining (eight tooth left).

Sir: Then you have lost eighty three.

Madam: Impossyble.

Sir: Everydobby knows there are foor decisives two canyons and ten grundies, which make thirsty ·two in all.

Madam: But I have done everything to save my tooth.

Sir: Perhumps! but to no avague.

Madam: Ah! why did I not insult you sooner?

Sir:　　To late, it must be now or neville.

Madam: You will pull it out for me then?

Sir:　　No, madman, I will excrete it.

Madam: But that is very painfull.

Sir:　　Let me see it – Crack! there it be madarce.

Madam: But sir I wished to keep (was anxious to keep)
　　　　 that tooth.

Sir:　　It was all black and moody, and the others are
　　　　 too.

Madam: Mercy – I will have none to eat with soon.

Sir:　　A free Nasty Heath set is good, and you will
　　　　 look thirty years jungle.

Madam: (Aside) Thirty years jungle; (Aloud) Sir I am no
　　　　 catholic, pull out all my stumps.

Sir:　　O.K. Gummy.

The Fat Growth on Eric Hearble

One fat morning Eric Hearble wake up with an abnorman fat growth a bombly on his head. 'Oh crumb,' said Eric Hearble, who was a very very, surprised. Anyway he carried on as Norman for why should he worried ? All of suddy he heard a small little voice calling him by name, 'Eric ... Eric Hearble ' it seemed to say though I couldn't say for sure.

That night the very same voice spoke saying 'Eric, I am a growth on your very head, help me, Eric.'

Soon Eric became very attached to his fat growth friend.

'Call me Scab,' the voice said and he was.

'Call me Eric,' Eric said naturly as he could. From then on you never saw Eric without the big fat scab growth on his head. And that's why Eric Hearble lost his job teaching spastics to dance.

'Were not having a cripple teaching our lads,' said Headmaster.

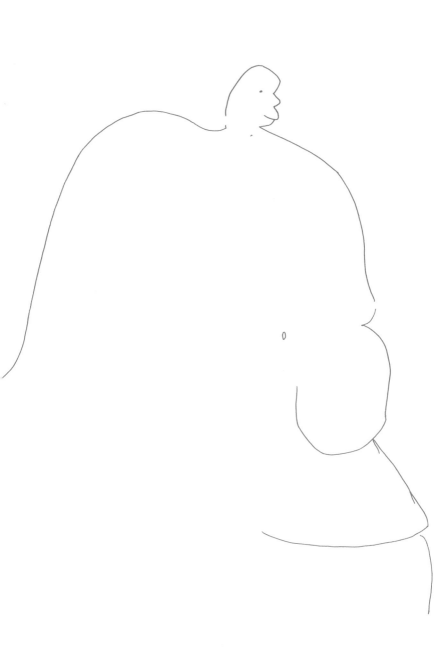

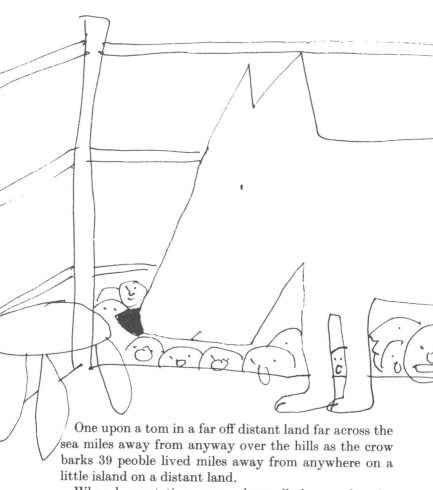

THE WRESTLING DOG

One upon a tom in a far off distant land far across the sea miles away from anyway over the hills as the crow barks 39 peoble lived miles away from anywhere on a little island on a distant land.

When harvest time came along all the people cele-brated with a mighty feast and dancing and that. It was

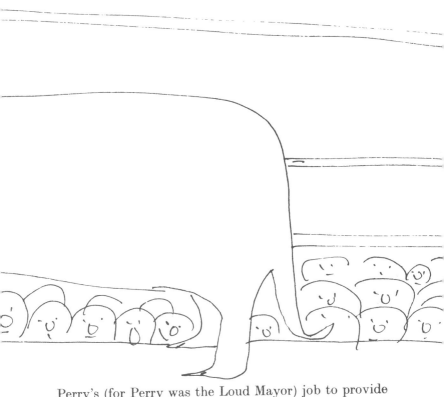

Perry's (for Perry was the Loud Mayor) job to provide
(and Perry's great pleasure I might add) a new and
exciting (and it usually was) thrill and spectacular per-
former (sometimes a dwarf was used), this year Perry
had surpassed himselve by getting a Wrestling Dog!
But who would fight this wondrous beast? I wouldn't
for a kick off.

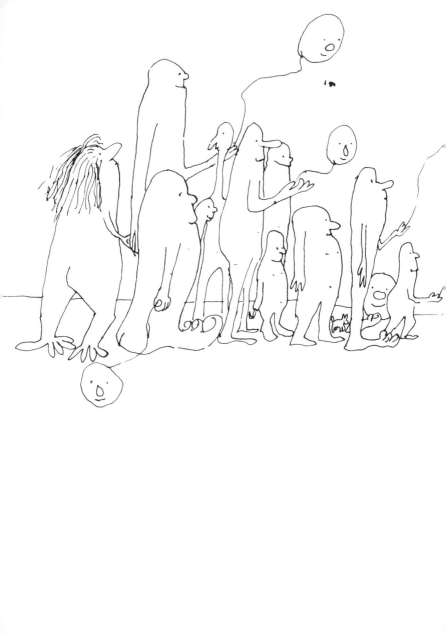

Randolf's Party

It was Chrisbus time but Randolph was alone. Where were all his good pals. Bernie, Dave, Nicky, Alice, Beddy, Freba, Viggy, Nigel, Alfred, Clive, Stan, Frenk, Tom, Harry, George, Harold? Where were they on this day? Randolf looged saggly at his only Chrispbut cart from his dad who did not live there.

'I can't understan this being so aloneley on the one day of the year when one would surely spect a pal or two?' thought Rangolf. Hanyway he carried on putting ub the desicrations and muzzle toe. All of a surgeon there was amerry timble on the door. Who but who could be a knocking on my door? He opend it and there standing there who? but only his pals. Bernie, Dave, Nicky, Alice, Beddy, Freba, Viggy, Nigel, Alfred, Clive, Stan, Frenk, Tom, Harry, George, Harolb weren't they?

Come on in old pals buddys and mates. With a big griff on his face Randoff welcombed them. In they came jorking and labbing shoubing 'Haddy Grimmble, Randoob.' and other hearty, and then they all jumbed on him and did smite him with mighty blows about his head crying, 'We never liked you all the years we've known you. You were never raelly one of us you know, soft head.'

They killed him you know, at least he didn't *die* alone did he? Merry Chrustchove, Randolf old pal buddy.

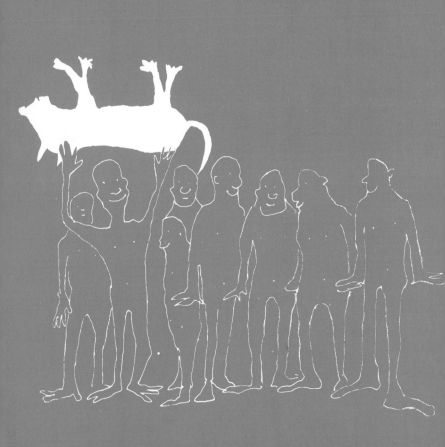

by the light of their faithful dog Cragesmure ...

The Famous Five

through Woenow Abbey

It was holliday time for the famous five by Enig Blyter; Tom, Stan, Dave, Nigel, Berniss, Arthur, Harry, Wee Jockey, Matoombo, and Craig? For the past 17 years the fabled fibe had been forming into adventures on varicose islands and secrete vallets with their famous ill bred dog, Cragesmure. Their popular Uncle Philpole with his popular curly white hair and his rugged red weather battered face and his popular fisherman's boots and his big junky sweater and his littel cottage.

'Gruddly Pod, Gruddly Pod,' the train seemed to say, 'Gruddly Pod, we're on our hollidays,' and they were. Pon arrival they noticed a mysterious stranger who bode no ill?

'Oi what's this 'ere,' he said from behind.

'We're the famous fire by Greenod Bladder,' replied Tom, Stan, Dave, Nigel, Berniss, Arthur, Harry, Wee Jocky, Matoombo, and Craig?, and they were.

'Don't you dare go on the mysterious Woenow Abbey Hill.'

That night by the light of their faithful dog Cragesmure, they talked Craig and Mtoombo into foing the dirty worj. Soon they were at Woenow Attlee grazine upone an olde crypped who turned round to be the furtive stranger.

'Keep off the grass,' he asked frae a great hat.

Matoombo sprange and soon overpowdered the old crypt with a half helsie. Craig ? quickly fried the old crypt together.

'Wart is the secrete of Woebeat Dobby ?' Craig ? asked.

'Yer can beat me but ne'er ye'll learn the secrete,' he answered from a green hut.

'Anything you say may be used in Everton against you,' said Harry. And it was.

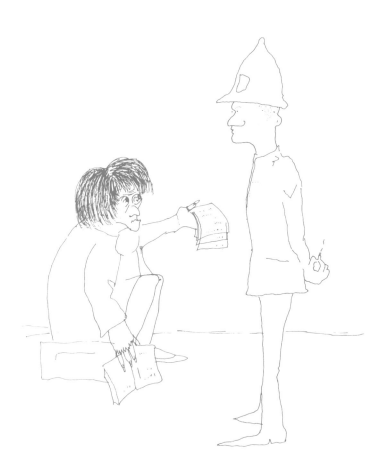

Sad Michael

There was no reason for Michael to be sad that morning, (the little wretch); everyone liked him, (the scab). He'd had a hard days night that day, for Michael was a Cocky Watchtower. His wife Bernie, who was well controlled, had wrabbed his norman lunch but he was still sad. It was strange for a man whom have everything and a wife to boot. At 4 o'clock when his fire was burking bridely a Poleaseman had clubbed in to parse the time around. 'Goodeven Michael,' the Poleaseman speeg, but Michael did not answer for he was debb and duff and could not speeg.

'How's the wive, Michael' spoge the Poleaseman

'Shuttup about that!'

'I thought you were debb and duff and could not speeg,' said the Poleaseman.

'Now what am I going to do with all my debb and duff books?' said Michael, realising straight away that here was a problem to be reckoned with.

I Wandered

On balmy seas and pernie schooners
On strivers and warming things
In a peanut coalshed clad
I wandered happy as a jew
To meet good Doris King.

Past grisby trees and hulky builds
Past ratters and bradder sheep
In a resus baby stooped
I wandered hairy as a dog
To get a goobites sleep

Down hovey lanes and stoney claves
Down ricketts and sticklys myth
In a fatty hebrew gurth
I wandered humply as a sock
To meet bad Bernie Smith

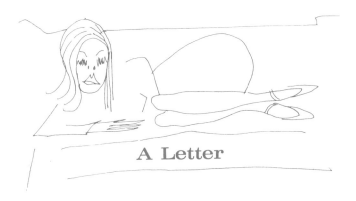

A Letter

Sir,

Why are there not more pidgers and writty about our favourit group (Berneese und zee Rippers). There are thirty-nine of them, you know. We like it cause Alec jumb about and shoes. Pleese send a stabbed undressed envelope of Bern and Ern dancing and doing their splendid to entertain a most deserting group and we hope this fires you as you keeler.

An admirrer.

Afan.

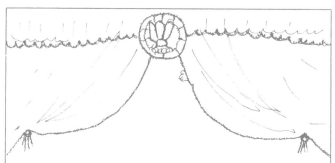

Scene three Act one

(*Scene*) *A broadshouldered room containing hugh fireplace facing a large big windy, a giant-size desk is covered in all type of many business paper and great disorder to look on. There are three or four or five chairs faceing the desk. One are occupied by a scruddy working clog, cap in hook what is gesticulated greatly but humble toward a big fat catipalyst boss. A white man carefully puts coal on the fire and steps back toward a giant door which seems to lead somewhere else. A cat smarting in the corner by the fire leaps up and smiles all on the carpet. A photy of Fieldimarcher Loud Montgammery solving a prodlem looks down on the two men, each of them looking up at it trying to place him.*

A dog is quietly gnawing at a pigmy under the giant desk. The time is half past three on the old grandbladder clock by the windy.

Fatty: 'It's harf parst three Taddpill, and the men
            haven't done a strike. Why can't we settle
            this here and now without resorting to a long
            union discussion and going through all that
            bit about your father.'

Scruddy: 'Why don't yer shut yer gob yer big fat get or
            I'll kick yer face in. Yer all the same you rich
            fat Bourgies, workin' uz poor workers to death
            and getting all the gelt and going to France
            for yer 'olidays.'

Fatty: (*going all red and ashen*)
            'But listen Taddpill you're only working two
            hours a day now, and three days a week and
            we're losing money as it is, and here you are
            complaining again about screw screwing and
            I'm trying to help you. We could have built
            our factory somewhere else where men like to
            work, but Ho no here we are goverment-
            sponsored and all that.'

Scruddy: 'Why don't yer shut yer gob yer big fat get
            or I'll kick yer face in. Yer all the same you
            rich fat Bourgies, workin' uz poor workers to
            death and getting all the gelt and going to
            France for yer 'holidays.'
            (*Enter a coloured woman singing a coloured
            song, On her back is a great bundle.*)

Mammy: 'Pope dat barge, left that bail'
            (*She unloads her bundle on the right of the desk.*)

Fatty: (*Impatiently*)
            'What is it Mammy, can't you see I'm haveing
            a prodlem with Taddpill and you come in
            here all black and singing? And get that

bundle of ruddish away from my big desk!'

Mammy: 'O.K. Kimu sahib bwana, massa'
(*she lifts the bundle and eats it*)
'Sho' was naice'

Fatty: 'Anyway what was it mammy?'

Mammy: 'Dat was yo' little daughter, by yo' secind wife KIMU SAHIB'

Fatty: (*colouring*)
'But I'm not married, old Mammy'

(*Mammy clasps her hands to her head horryfried*)
'Oh Lord, I've jes' eaten a bastard!'

(*She runs round the room crossing herself, and singing another verse. Scruddy stands up replaceing his cap firmly on his head – walking toward the door he half turns like in the films and shakes his fist.*)

'Get this black woman out of this factory before the men find out, or yer'll 'ave a strike on yer fat Bourgie 'ands. I'm tellin yer that fer nothin' yer old bum!'

(*Scruddy walks out of the room leaving Fatty – Mammy and fourteen little Jewish children all singing together a kind of hymn.*)

The End

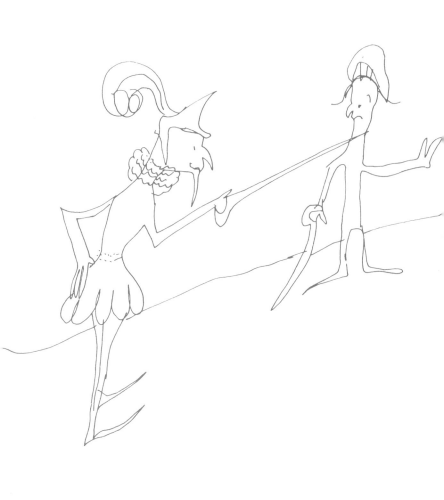

Treasure Ivan

In a little seashore pub in Bristow, a ragged gathering of rags are drinking and makeing melly (before sailing to sea in serge of grate treashy on a sudden Isle far across the ocean).

'Belay there me 'earty scabs,' says Large John Saliver entering. Pegging along towards some old saviours whom have soled the several seas.

'Where be the Parable you normally 'ave on your shoulder, Large John?' Asks Blind Jew looking up.

'Never ye mind' reponds Large John 'And anyways where be your white stick?'

''Ow the 'ell should I know when oi can't see?'

All of a suddy Small Jack Hawkins creep in unobtrugell with a siddy grip on his head.

'Ha ha aa aar Jack lad' says Large John in a typical

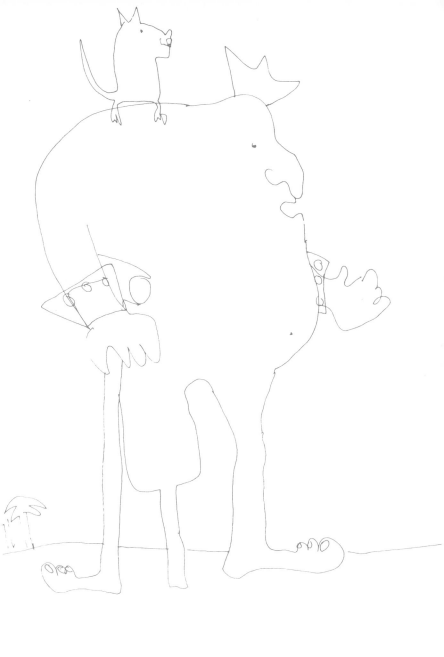

mariner marino.

Soon they were heady fir the harboar with Cpt Smellit and Squire Trelorgy. That morgan they sailed with a hearty breeze behind.

Large John began to look upon Jack as a son or something, for he was ever putting his arm about him and saying 'Ha Haaaaar', especially with a Parable on his shouldy. One day, however, Small Jack Hawkins was just happening in a barret of abbeys when he over-heated Large John and several other saviours planting to botany against the Captain.

'Lung Ho' cry a voice from the pidgeon tow on high, 'Lung Ho and alls well!' Yes and it were true – a little Ivan, cyril carpet agaist the horivan with palmist trees and cockynuts.

'I wouldn't be suprised if there was not a beardy old man hobbing from rock to rock.' Thought Disreali Hands who'd seen the film, and there was.

The first lungboot ashore contained Large John Saliver Small Jack and some others what were numerous and sweaty to behold. Anyway they landed on the Ivan and an owld loon jumps out calling himself Sten Gunn and he's been living all over the treasure for years because cruel old Captaive Flint has put the Black Pot on him and you know what happens with a black pot.

So after a bit of stockade and that they sail home to Bristow where they're all arrested for development and Jack Hawkins turns round to be a thirty two year old midget and Large John Saliver has to pay for a new woody leg because they run from fireplace on the Ivan. Sten Gunn turns round to be a young man in the prime of minister and Tom the faithful cat returns to Newcastle.

All Abord Speeching

1. Speak you Clear and Nasal, for distance.
   '*Ron cordially begs to inform Mam all is forgiven.*'
   Many peoble express great height with the word
   Mam.

2. Sing you with long voice.
   For discharge
   Deep breathing is Nescafe for a dark voice, deep
   breeding and in haley is very impotent for broad-
   castle and outlying ariels ... visibility nil in Rockall
   and Fredastaire? Practice daily but not if you're
   debb and duff.

3. For sample, the word frenetically wrote, must be
   charged grammactically with bowel pronouned
   strangley.
   eg. '*While talking on you my Ivans are getting cold,
   and you know, as well as I do, that we must strive the
   Ivan while it is hat.*'
   Regarth in Oxfam they speak '*Aivan*' but in Caim-
   bilge '*Oivan*' – the bowel thus strethed pronuned –
   piglo.
   Practice davy but not if your Mutt and Jeff.

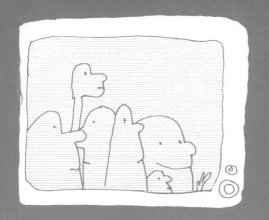

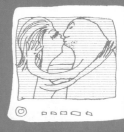

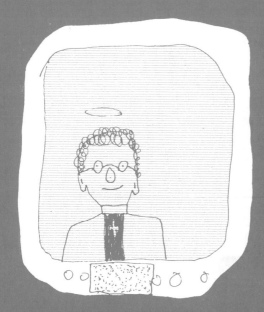

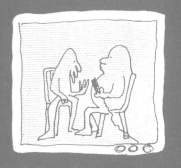

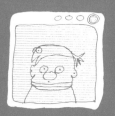

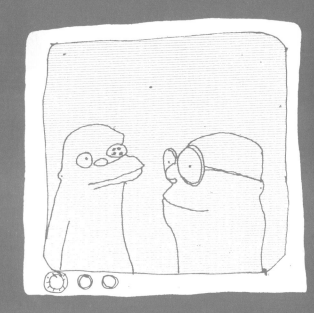

THE FINGLETOAD RESORT

OF

TEDDIVISCIOUS

PECKLE AND BRACES (GRANARTHUR)

How many body peoble wash 'Peotle and Plaices'? In a recent Doddipottiddy Poll a roaming retorter intervined asking –

'*Do you like Big Grunty better more than Gray Burk*'?

To these questiump many people answered

'*On the other hand who are we to judge? I mean who are we*'?

PANORASTHMA (BBC)

The self same questium was asked through some more kind worjing folk about –

'*Do you prepare Rinkled Dinglebone or Tichie Bimplebean*'?

To this inquest many people answering.

'*Who the hell is Pimpled Dinkletoes? Anyway Who is he?*'

THIS DISPROVES THE PILTDOWN RETORD THAT:

a) Their all washing the rabio.

b) Are their too many adversements on I.T.B.? That seems to be the crutch of the matter. As far as I'm conceived they're foing a grate jobe. But retarding the BBBC's Doddumental Frogrammes – excelent even if they say so theyselfs.

c) $9\frac{1}{2}$ peodle wash I.T.B.

And they wash BBBBC. Every bodypeogle else read the Deadly Excess or the Davey Grail, except Godfree Wind.

Alec Speaking

He is putting it lithely when he says

Quobble in the Grass,

Strab he down the soddieflays

Amo amat amass;

Amonk amink a minibus,

Amarmylaidie Moon,

Amikky mendip multiplus

Amighty midgey spoon.

And so I traddled onward

Careing not a care

Onward, Onward, Onward.

Onward, my friends to victory and glory for the thirtyninth.

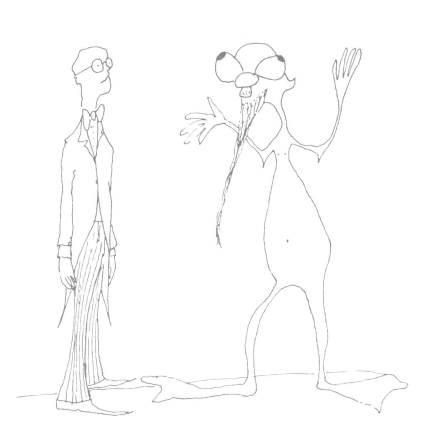

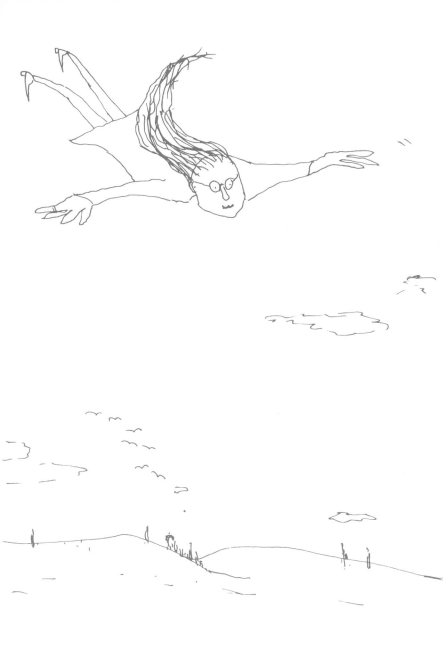

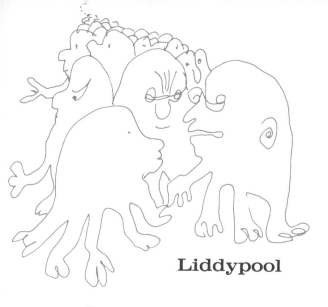

Liddypool

Reviving the old tradition of Judro Bathing is slowly but slowly dancing in Liddypool once more. Had you remembering these owld custard of Boldy Street blowing? The Peer Hat is very popularce for sun eating and Boots for Nude Brighter is handys when sailing. We are not happy with her Queen Victorious Monologue, but Walky Through Gallery is goodly when the rain and Sit Georgie House is black (and white from the little pilgrims flying from Hellsy College). Talk Hall is very histerical with old things wot are fakes and King Anne never slept there I tell you. Shout Airborne is handly for planes if you like (no longer government patrolled) and the L.C.C.C. (Liddypool Cha Cha Cha) are doing a great thing. The Mersey Boat is selling another three copies to some go home foreigners who went home.

There is a lot to do in Liddypool, but not all convenience.

You Might Well Arsk

Why were Prevelant ze Gaute, unt Docker Adenoid getting so friendly? You might well arsk. Why was Seldom Loyled sagged? Why did Harrassed MacMillion go golphing mit Bod Hobe? Why is Frank Cunnings and and the T.U.C. against the Commen Margate? You might well arsk. Why is the Duck of Edincalvert a sailing mit Udda Fogs? Why did Priceless Margarine unt Bony Armstrove give Jamaika away? You might well arsk. Why won't Friendly Trumap give his Captive his pension.

Nicely Nicely Clive

To Clive Barrow it was just an ordinary day nothing unusual or strange about it, everything quite navel, nothing outstanley just another day but. to Roger it was somthing special, a day amongst days ... a red lettuce day ... because Roger was getting married and as he dressed that morning he thought about the gay batchelor soups he'd had with all his pals. And Clive said nothing. To Roger everything was different, wasn't this the day his Mother had told him about, in his best suit and all that, grimming and shakeing hands, people tying boots and ricebudda on his car.

To have and to harm ... till death duty part ... he knew it all off by hertz. Clive Barrow seemed oblivious. Roger could visualise Anne in her flowing weddy drag, being wheeled up the aisle, smiling a blessing. He had butterfield in his stomarce as he fastened his bough tie and brushed his hairs. 'I hope I'm doing the right thing' he thought looking in the mirror, 'Am I good enough for her?' Roger need not have worried because he was 'Should I have flowers all round the spokes?' said Anne polishing her foot rest. 'Or should I keep it syble?' she continued looking down on her grain haired Mother.

'Does it really matter?' repaid her Mother wearily wiping her sign. 'He won't be looking at your spokes anyway.' Anne smiled the smile of someone who's seen a few laughs.

Then luckily Anne's father came home from sea and cancelled the husband.

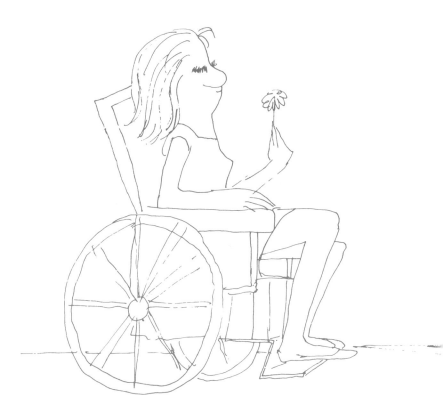

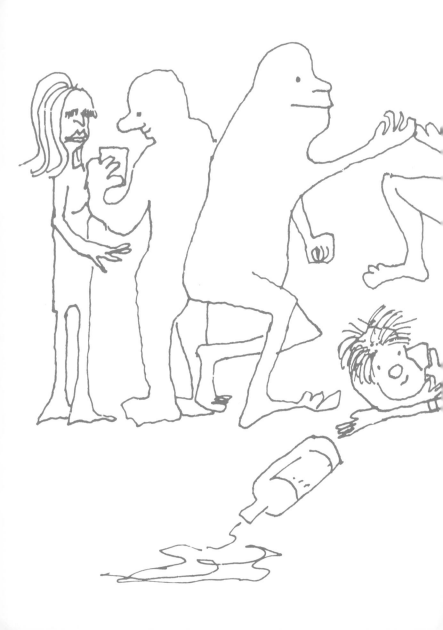

Puffing and globbering they drugged theyselves rampling or dancing with wild abdomen, stubbing in wild postumes amongst themselves ...

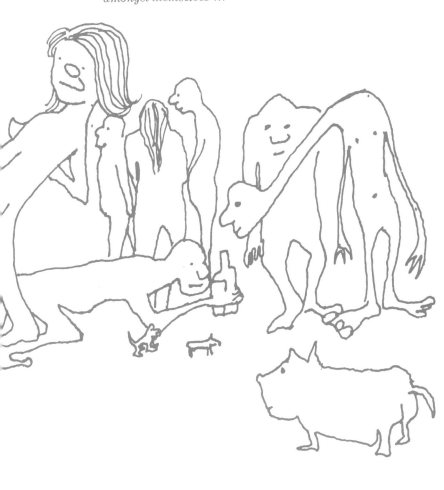

Neville Club

Dressed in my teenold brown sweaty I easily micked with crown at Neville Club a seemy hole. Soon all but soon people accoustic me saying such thing as

'Where the charge man?' All of a southern I notice boils and girks sitting in hubbered lumps smoking Hernia taking Odeon and going very high. Somewhere 4ft high but he had Indian Hump which he grew in his sleep. Puffing and globbering they drugged theyselves rampling or dancing with wild abdomen, stubbing in wild postumes amongst themselves.

They seemed olivier to the world about them. One girk was revealing them all over the place to rounds of bread and applause. Shocked and mazed I pulled on my rubber stamp heady for the door.

'Do you kindly mind stop shoveing,' a brough voice said.

'Who think you are?' I retired smiling wanly.

'I'm in charge,' said the brough but heavy voice.

'How high the moon?' cried another, and the band began to play.

A coloured man danced by eating a banana, or somebody.

I drudged over hopping to be noticed. He iced me warily saying 'French or Foe'.

'Foe' I cried taking him into jeapardy.

The Moldy Moldy Man

I'm a moldy moldy man
I'm moldy thru and thru
I'm a moldy moldy man
You would not think it true.
I'm moldy till my eyeballs
I'm moldy til my toe
I will not dance I shyballs
I'm such a humble Joe.

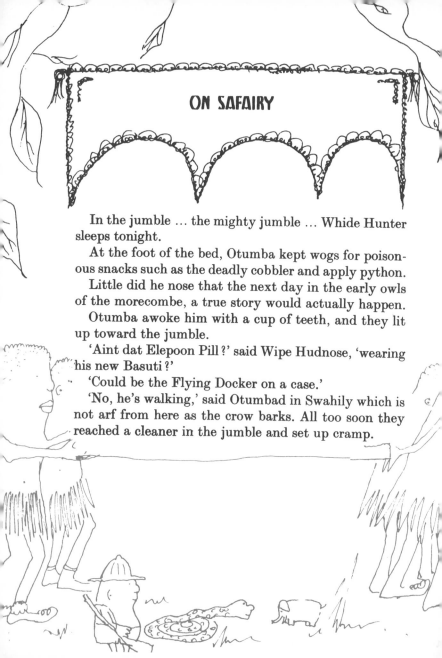

ON SAFAIRY

In the jumble ... the mighty jumble ... Whide Hunter sleeps tonight.

At the foot of the bed, Otumba kept wogs for poisonous snacks such as the deadly cobbler and apply python.

Little did he nose that the next day in the early owls of the morecombe, a true story would actually happen.

Otumba awoke him with a cup of teeth, and they lit up toward the jumble.

'Aint dat Elepoon Pill?' said Wipe Hudnose, 'wearing his new Basuti?'

'Could be the Flying Docker on a case.'

'No, he's walking,' said Otumbad in Swahily which is not arf from here as the crow barks. All too soon they reached a cleaner in the jumble and set up cramp.

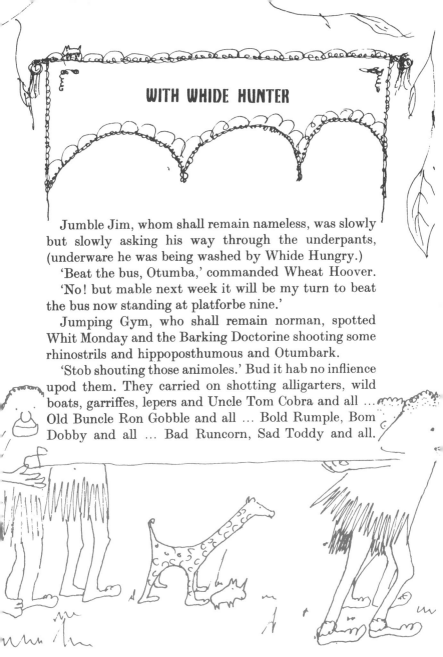

WITH WHIDE HUNTER

Jumble Jim, whom shall remain nameless, was slowly but slowly asking his way through the underpants, (underware he was being washed by Whide Hungry.)

'Beat the bus, Otumba,' commanded Wheat Hoover.

'No! but mable next week it will be my turn to beat the bus now standing at platforbe nine.'

Jumping Gym, who shall remain norman, spotted Whit Monday and the Barking Doctorine shooting some rhinostrils and hippoposthumous and Otumbark.

'Stob shouting those animoles.' Bud it hab no inflience upod them. They carried on shotting alligarters, wild boats, garriffes, lepers and Uncle Tom Cobra and all ... Old Buncle Ron Gobble and all ... Bold Rumple, Bom Dobby and all ... Bad Runcorn, Sad Toddy and all.

I Sat Belonely

I sat belonely down a tree,
humbled fat and small.
A little lady sing to me
I couldn't see at all.

I'm looking up and at the sky,
to find such wondrous voice.
Puzzly puzzle, wonder why,
I hear but have no choice.

'Speak up, come forth, you ravel me',
I potty menthol shout.
'I know you hiddy by this tree'.
But still she won't come out.

Such softly singing lulled me sleep,
an hour or two or so
I wakeny slow and took a peep
and still no lady show.

Then suddy on a little twig
I thought I see a sight,
A tiny little tiny pig,
that sing with all it's might.

'I thought you were a lady'.
I giggle, – well I may,
To my suprise the lady,
got up – and flew away.

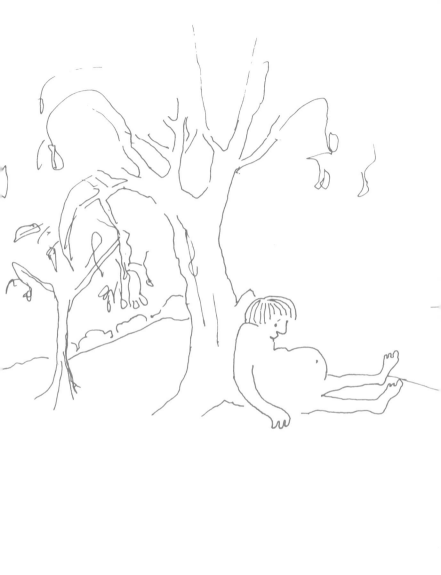

Henry and Harry

Henry was his father's son and it were time for him to leave school and go into him father's business of Brummer Striving. It wert a farst dying trade which was fast dying.

'But Brummer Striving is a farst dying business, Father,' said young Henry, a young lad. His dad, Harry replied quickly.

'None of thy nonsence, Henry. All thy fathers before-have and before even that before me were Brummers and that's a fact.' With that he pulled his stumps nearer the fire.

'Tell me again father about how you got those prize stumps was it not with a Brummer Towdry?' said young teenage Henry.

'Why do you always ask about my stumps, Son,' said Harry to Penry with a reasurring.

'Because it's a story I love to hear, Father – and besides it's not every one what has a real cripple for a father.'

'There's something in what you say, I dare say,' said Henry eyeing his son proudly; thinking. 'My son's a Brummer if I ever saw one,' and he had.

'I want to be a golfer, Dad,' said Henry hopefully without a laugh.

'You're a Brummer, Son, so get it straight,' said dad Harry.

The next day Henry could not be seen or heard about the quaint little slum and dad Harry was beginning to worry. 'It's not like him, Mother,' he said to a right old hag who was living with them.

'Blast his hide,' said mother, with an accent.

As you might have guessed, teenage young Henry had run around from home and left.

'I'll show that stump,' said Henry to himself, for there was no one with him. Well, it just so happened man that teenage young Henry could not get a golfing job anywhere especially Golfing.

'It seems I'm a born Brummer like dad Harry says I am,' said Harry quietly for no one was listening to him. So he humbled his way homeward like any other teenage Henry would who couldn't get a golfing job. He spotted the slum of his childhood and said out loud 'Crub' which put it in a nutshell.

'Mother, Mother, it's me, teenage young Henry, I'm home,' he said hopeing to be noticed. But hag mother just kept on digging as if she had not noticed him and she hadn't. 'Mother, Mother, it's me' he said repeating himself whilst thinking – 'I wonder what she's digging, it can't be the sounds man.' Still the old wretch kept on digging and also singing to herself – a song you don't often hear now a days. 'Mother, Mother,' said peristant teenage Henry, who was beginning to be a bit of a drag.

'Can't you see I'm burying Soft Harry, your father.' said hag Mother at last.

'All I wanted was a civil answer,' replied Henry assuming responsibility.

Deaf Ted, Danoota, (and me)

Thorg hilly grove and burly ive,
Big daleys grass and tree
We clobber ever gallup
Deaf Ted, Danoota, and me.

Never shall we partly stray,
Fast stirrup all we three
Fight the battle mighty sword
Deaf Ted, Danoota, and me.

With faithful frog beside us,
Big mighty club are we
The battle scab and frisky dyke
Deaf Ted, Danoota, and me.

We fight the baddy baddies,
For colour, race and cree
For Negro, Jew and Bernie
Deaf Ted, Danoota, and me.

Thorg Billy grows and Burnley ten,
And Aston Villa three
We clobber ever gallup
Deaf Ted, Danoota and me.

So if you hear a wonderous sight,
Am blutter or at sea,
Remember whom the mighty say
Deaf Ted, Danoota, and me –
(sometimes we bring our friend, Malcolm.)

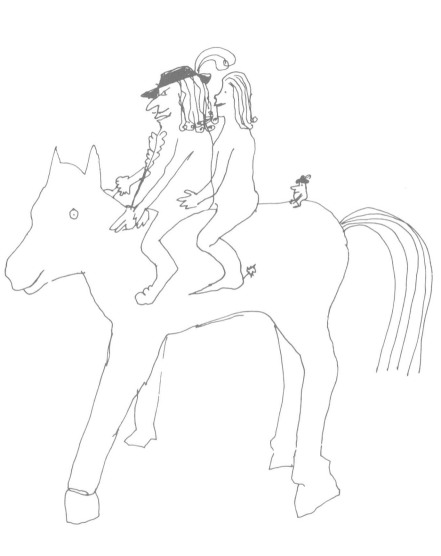

A Surprise for Little Bobby

It was little Bobby's birthmark today and he got a suprise. His very fist was jopped off, (The War) and he got a birthday hook!

All his life Bobby had wanted his very own hook; and now on his 39th birthday his pwayers had been answered. The only trouble was they had send him a left hook and ebry dobby knows that it was Bobby's right fist that was missing as it were.

What to do was not thee only problem: Anyway he jopped off his lest hand and it fitted like a glove. Maybe next year he will get a right hook, who knows?

Halbut Returb

(A Play)

Fourteen yearz now I halb been wading for sweet Halbut to return from the wars (little does she know Halbut Hare returbs suddenly to make an honest womb of her.)

H : 'Aim home Rosebeen, from the war y'know.'

R : 'Did yow git thee butter Halbot?'

H : 'Ai've brort ya a negru Rosebeen from the war y'know.'

R : 'For me my very own for me Halbot?'

H : 'Ai was always thinking on you Razebeem my own.'

R : 'Show me this very negru Helbout from the war, this is really living.'

H : 'No'.

R : 'What strange grurth has taken you Halford, am I not your very own?'

Unhappy Frank

Frank looked at the table hardly daring to look at the table.

'I hate that table,' he said 'Bloody owld table in my house.' Then he looked at the clock. 'Damn that clock in my house,' said Frank, for it was his house you know. After a little bit his eye came across his very mother's chair. 'Don't like that chair one bit,' he showbedy. 'Just look at that garbet all filby and durby. How am I supposed to look affaffter all this garby ruddish. Wart am I but a slave tow look upon with deesekfrebit all the peegle larfing and buzing me in front of all the worled. How can I but garry on? How? Hab I no live of my own to do but wart I must ever jub gleenig and looking areftor theese damn owld house of my own?' Frank went over to his dubb old mother, whomn was stikl liffing with him. 'What are you larfing at you dubb owld boot?'

'Havn' I nuff treble without you kakking in the korber?' With that Frank stub up and kicked her plainly on the head. 'Take that for larfing you budd oled griff.' 'I hate that boot,' he said smiling quirkley to themselves.

'I'm going to sell this daft shed and you to aswell, also Mummy.'

So he sold it all and left the country and settled down in another country which he did not like half as much as his dear old home in England with his dear old quaint old luvly mother what he (Frank) lost due to a bad harvest. Which judd go to show what happens.

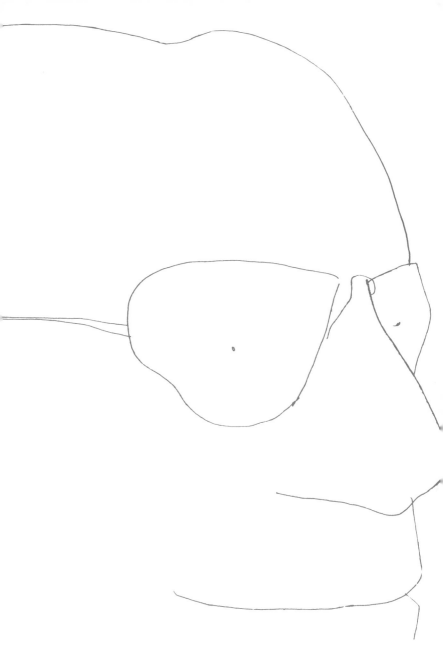

On this Churly Morn

Small wonder on this churly morn
I crivy like a black
To think wot I should be farlorn
Through knorb this packymack

I may be blink down booltoad
With ne'er a thorty skive
But I'll december barrold
To save my good bad Ive

To them perhap be nicky
I smirk but querry jump
With all this alfy hicky
I do but strive a hump

Knock down ye smallish hoqky
Am I the bairly oat?
With all your davey cockey
I'll always keep afloat.

Will I the baggy Dutch man
And haughty bygraves too
To all I give a limpage
To do what they will do.

They rabble till they're tatter
Don't creem the midnight hour
Big Doris flitter flatter
And blacky blackpoo tower

Rephy graun and gratty
Graddie large but smail
She will not brant a fatty
Room to swig a snail

Bilt zeitung dairy apple
Of geltzie sniedypye
Groppy gribble grapple
Varoum the reason why?

Ye bottle ginny derick
And all who sail without
My tall but little Eric
Shall ne'er but cast a clout!

Remplenish thou thy cravie
With all that bodes within
Fall gather barge and davie
The lamb within a bin.

God Speed

69

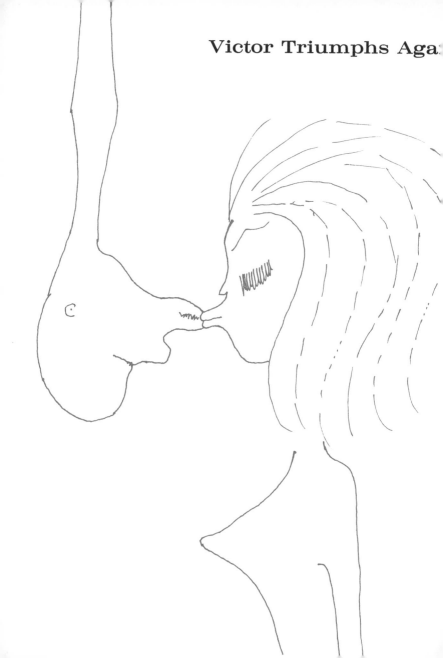

d Mrs. Weatherby Learns a Lesson

It were a small village, Squirmly on the Slug, and vile ruperts spread fat and thick amongst the inhabidads what libed there.

One victor of these gossipity tongues had oft been Victor Hardly, a harmless boot, whom never halmed nobody. A typical quimmty old hag who spread these vile ruperts was Mrs Weatherby – a widow by her first husbands.

'They're holding a Black Matt down at Victors pad,' was oft heard about the village – but I never heard it. Things like this were getting Victor down, if not lower.

'Why but why do they say these bad thing about me when I have but never halmed or speak bad,' he would say, but I never heard him.

'He's drawing bad Christians on the graves,' Mrs Weatherby would spread. The whole village was alarming.

'We can't have all this,' said the Vicar, who was a Christian. 'We'll have to set a trap and catch this fowl fiend what desicated our church.'

Once and forearm plans were made to prove who it were playing the Darryl with the church. On Thursday or Monday a little group of thirty-two people, all dictionaries of the Counsil, and the Parcel and the Vicar all hid noticeably amongst all the other dead things lying about.

'This will catch him, God willy,' thought a man with Oxfam on his face.

After eight hours or so they all noticed that nothing had happened – and they began to wonder – why? after all hadn't they had the information from a reliable sore?

I Remember Arnold

I remember Kakky Hargreaves
As if 'twer Yestermorn'
Kakky, Kakky Hargreaves
Son of Mr. Vaughan.

He used to be so grundie
On him little bike
Riding on a Sundie
Funny little tyke

Yes, I remember Kathy Hairbream
As if 'twer yesterday
Katthy, Kathy Hairbream
Son of Mr. May

Arriving at the station
Always dead on time
For his destination
Now He's dead on line
(meaning he's been got by a train or something)

And so we growt and bumply
Till the end of time,
Humpty dumpty bumply
Son of Harry Lime.

> *Bumbleydy Hubledy Humbley*
> *Bumdley Tum. (Thank you)*

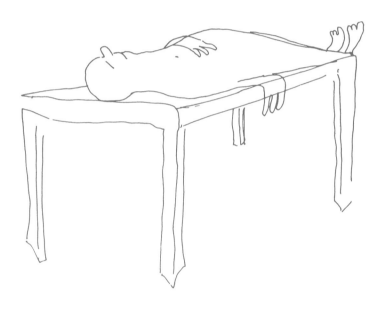

JOHN LENNON

A SPANIARD IN THE WORKS

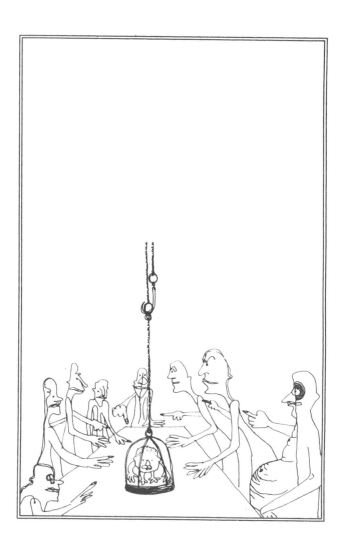

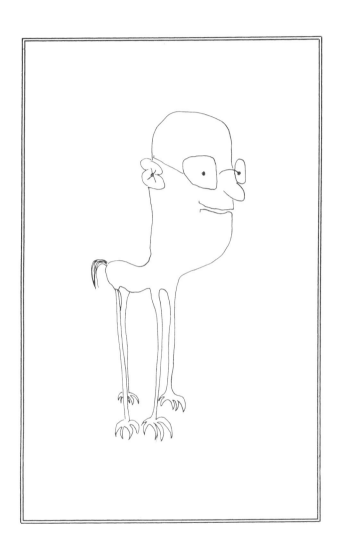

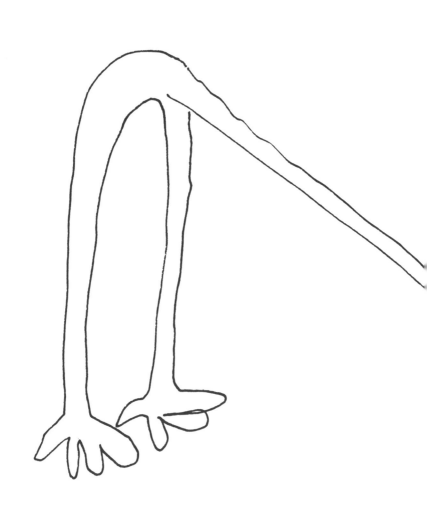

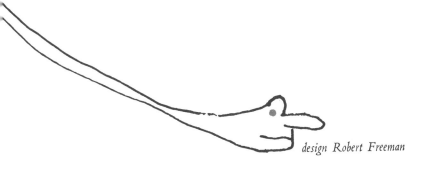
design Robert Freeman

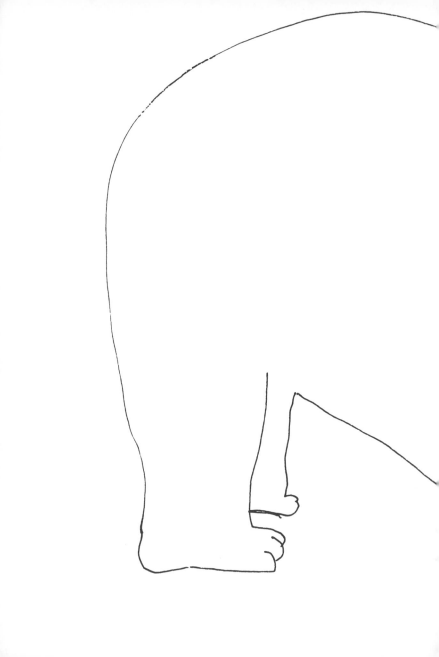

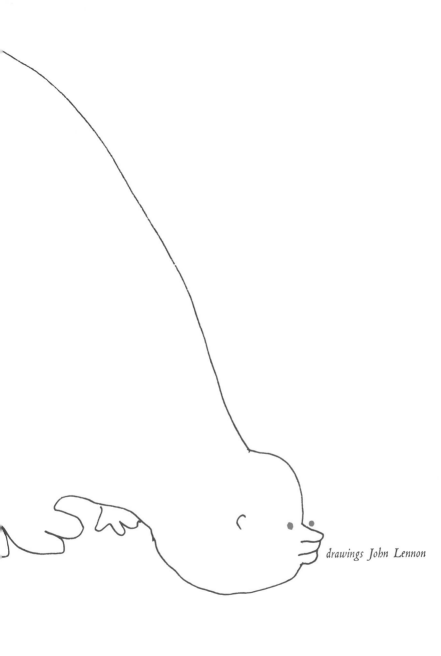

drawings John Lennon

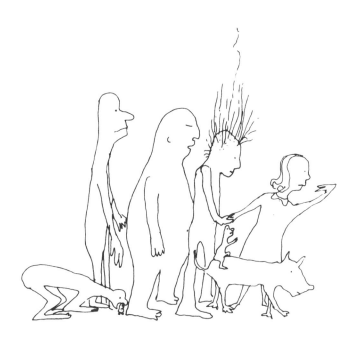

CONTENTS

A Spaniard in the Works   87

The Fat Budgie   92

Snore Wife and some Several Dwarts   96

The Singularge Experience of Miss Anne Duffield   98

The Faulty Bagnose   108

We must not forget the General Erection   114

Benjaman Distasteful   116

The Wumberlog (or The Magic Dog)   118

Araminta Ditch   127

Cassandle   134

The National Health Cow   136

Readers Lettuce   138

Silly Norman   140

Mr. Boris Morris   144

Bernice's Sheep   146

Last Will and Testicle   150

Our Dad   157

I Believe, Boot...   162

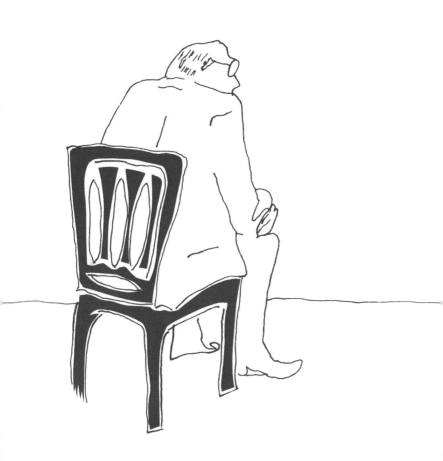

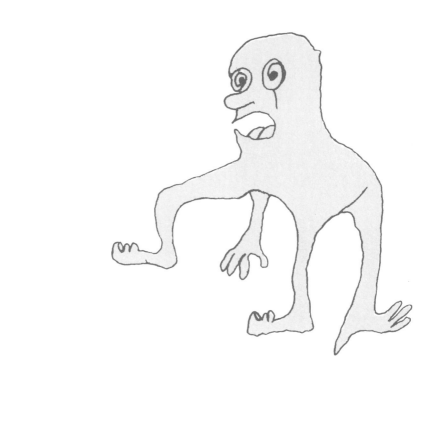

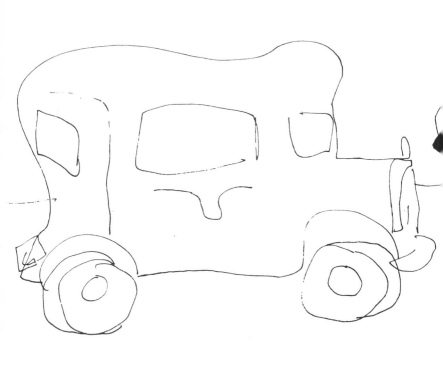

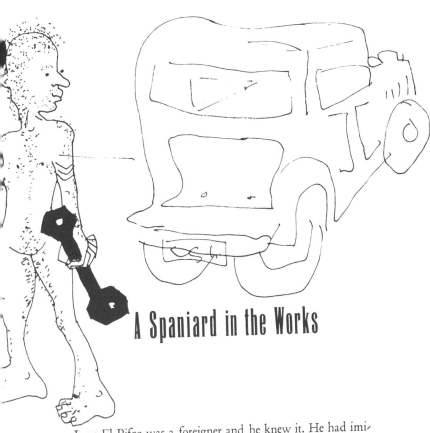

A Spaniard in the Works

Jesus El Pifco was a foreigner and he knew it. He had imigrateful from his little white slum in Barcelover a good thirsty year ago having first secured the handy job as coachman in Scotland. The job was with the Laird of McAnus, a canny old tin whom have a castle in the Highlads. The first thing Jesus El Pifco noticed in early the days was that the Laird didn't seem to have a coach of any discription or even a coach house you know, much to his dismable. But – and I use the word lightly – the Laird did seem to having some horses, each one sporting a fine pair of legs. Jesus fell in love with them at first sight, as they did with him, which was lucky, because his quarters were in the actually stables along side his noble four lepered friends.

Pretty polly one could see Jesus almost every day, grooming his masters horses, brushing their manebits and hammering their teeth, whistling a quaint Spanish refrain dreaming of his loved wombs back home in their little white fascist bastard huts.

'A well pair of groomed horses I must say,' he would remark to wee Spastic Sporran the flighty chamberlain, whom he'd had his good eye on eversince Hogmanose.

'Nae sa bad' she would answer in her sliced Aberdeen martin accent. 'Ye spend more time wi' yon horses than ye do wi' me,' with that she would storm back to her duties, carefully tying her chastity negro hardly to her skim.

Being a good catholic, Jesus wiped the spit from his face and turned the other cheese – but she had gone leaving him once small in an agatha of christy.

'One dave she woll go too farther, and I woll leaf her' he said to his fave rave horse. Of course the horse didn't answer, because as you know they cannot speak, least of all to a garlic eating, stinking, little yellow greasy fascist bastard catholic Spaniard. They soon made it up howevans and Jesus and wee Spastic were once morphia unitely in a love that knew no suzie. The only thing that puzzled Jesus was why his sugarboot got so annoyed when he called her his little Spastic in public.

Little wonder howeapon, with her real name being Patrick, you see?

'Ye musna' call me Spastic whilst ma friends are here Jesus ma bonnie wee dwarf' she said irragated.

'But I cannot not say Patrick me little tartan bag' he replied all herb and angie inside. She looked down at him through a mass of naturally curly warts.

'But Spastic means a kind of cripple in English ma sweet wee Jesus, and ai'm no cripple as you well known!'

'That's true enough' said he 'but I didn't not realize being a foreigner and that, and also not knowing your countries culture and so force, and anywait I can spot a cripple anywhere.'

He rambled on as Patrick knelt down lovingly with tears in her eye and slowly bit a piece of his bum. Then lifting her face upwarts, she said with a voice full of emulsion 'Can ye heffer forgive me Jesus, can ye?' she slobbed. He looked at her strangely as if she were a strangely, then taking her slowly right foot he cried; 'Parreesy el pino a strevaro qui bueno el franco senatro!' which rugby transplanted means – 'Only if you've got green braces' – and fortunately she had.

They were married in the fallout, with the Lairds blessing of course, he also gave them a 'wee gifty' as he put it, which was a useful addition to their bottom lawyer. It was a special jar of secret ointment made by generators of his forefingers to help get rid of Patricks crabs which she had unluckily caught from the Laird of McAnus himself at his late wifes (Lady McAnus') wake. They were overjoyced, and grapenut abun and beyond the call of duty.

'The only little crawlie things we want are babies,' quipped Jesus who was a sport. 'That's right sweety' answered Patrick reaching for him with a knowsley hall.

'Guid luck to you and yours' shouted the Laird from the old wing.

'God bless you sir' said Jesus quickly harnessing his wife with a dexterity that only practice can perfect. 'Come on me beauty' he whispered as he rode his wife at a steady trot towards the East Gate. 'We mustn't miss the first race my dear.'

'Not likely' snorted his newly wed wife breaking into a gullup. 'Not likely' she repeated.

The honeymood was don short by a telephant from Mrs El Pifco (his mother) who was apparently leaving Barcelunder to see her eldest sod febore she died laughing, and besides the air would do her good she added. Patrick looked up from her nosebag and giggled.

'Don't joke about Mamma please if you donlang, she are all I have loft in the world and besides your mother's a bit of a brockwürst herselves' said Jesus, 'And if she's still alive when she gets here we can throw up a party for her and then she can meet all our ugly Scottish friends' he reflected. 'On the other handle we can always use her as a scarecrab in the top field' said Patrick practically.

So they packed their suitcrates marked 'his and hearse' and set off for their employers highly home in the highlies.

'We're home Sir' said Jesus to the wizened tartan figure knelt crouching over a bag of sheep.

'Why are ye bask so soon?' inquired the Laird, immediately recognizing his own staff through years of experience. 'I've had some bad jews from my Mammy – she's coming to seagull me, if its all ripe with you sir.' The Laird thought for a mumble, then his face lit up like a boiling wart.

'You're all fired' he smiled and went off whistling.

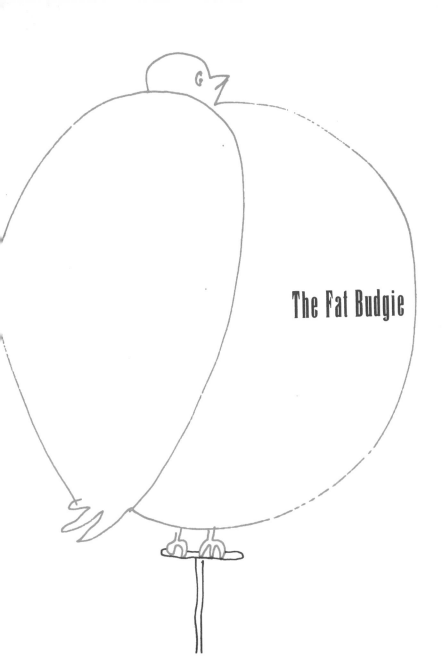

The Fat Budgie

I have a little budgie
He is my very pal
I take him walks in Britain
I hope I always shall.

I call my budgie Jeffrey
My grandads name's the same
I call him after grandad
Who had a feathered brain.

Some people don't like budgies
The little yellow brats
They eat them up for breakfast
Or give them to their cats.

My uncle ate a budgie
It was so fat and fair.
I cried and called him Ronnie
He didn't seem to care

Although his name was Arthur
It didn't mean a thing.
He went into a petshop
And ate up everything.

The doctors looked inside him,
To see what they could do,
But he had been too greedy
He died just like a zoo.

My Jeffrey chirps and twitters
When I walk into the room,
I make him scrambled egg on toast
And feed him with a spoon.

He sings like other budgies
But only when in trim
But most of all on Sunday
Thats when I plug him in.

He flies about the room sometimes
And sits upon my bed
And if he's really happy
He does it on my head.

He's on a diet now you know
From eating far too much
They say if he gets fatter
He'll have to wear a crutch.

It would be funny wouldn't it
A budgie on a stick
Imagine all the people
Laughing till they're sick.

So that's my budgie Jeffrey
Fat and yellow too
I love him more than daddie
And I'm only thirty two.

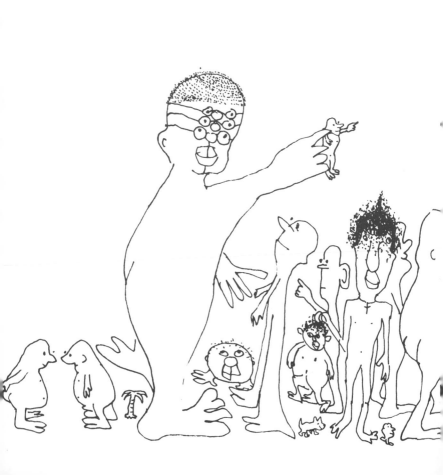

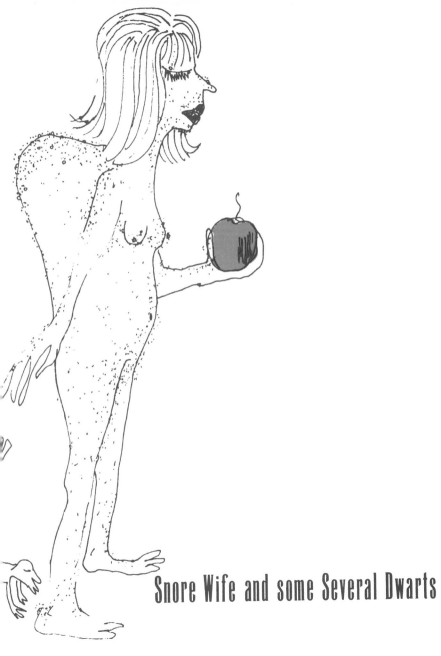

Snore Wife and some Several Dwarts

Once upon upon in a dizney far away – say three hundred year agoal if you like – there lived a sneaky forest some several dwarts or cretins; all named – Sleezy, Grumpty, Sneeky, Dog, Smirkey, Alice? Derick – and Wimpey. Anyway they all dug about in a diamond mind, which was rich beyond compère. Every day when they came hulme from wirk, they would sing a song – just like ordinary wirkers – the song went something like – 'Yo ho! Yo ho! it's off to wirk we go!' – which is silly really considerable they were comeing hulme. (Perhaps ther was slight housework to be do.)

One day howitzer they (Dwarts) arrived home, at aprodestant six o'cloth, and who? – who do they find? – but only Snore Wife, asleep in Grumpty's bed. He didn't seem to mine. 'Sambody's been feeding *my* porrage!' screams Wimpey, who was wearing a light blue pullover. Meanwife in a grand Carstle, not so mile away, a womand is looging in her daily mirror, shouting, 'Mirror mirror on the wall, whom is de fairy in the land.' which doesn't even rhyme. 'Cassandle!' answers the mirror. 'Chrish O'Malley' studders the womand who appears to be a Queen or a witch or an acorn.

'She's talking to that mirror again farther?' says Misst Cradock, 'I've just seen her talking to that mirror again.' Father Cradock turns round slowly from the book he is eating and explains that it is just a face she is going through and they're all same at that age. 'Well I don't like it one tit,' continhughs Misst Cradock. Father Cradock turns round slowly from the book he is eating, explaining that she doesn't have to like it, and promptly sets fire to his elephant. 'Sick to

96

death of this elephant I am,' he growls, 'sick to death of it eating like an elephant all over the place.'

Suddenly bark at the Several Dwarts home, Snore Wife has became a *firm favourite*, especially with her helping arm, brushing away the little droppings. 'Good old Snore Wife!' thee all sage, 'Good old Snore Wife is our fave rave.' 'And I like you tooth!' rejoices Snore Wife, 'I like you all my little dwarts.' Without warping they hear a soddy voice continuallykhan shoubing and screeging about apples for sale. 'New apples for old!' says the above hearing voice. 'Try these nice new apples for chris, sake!' Grumpy turnips quick and answers shooting – 'Why?' and they all look at him.

A few daisy lately the same voice comes hooting aboon the apples for sale with a rarther more firm aproach saying 'These apples are definitely for sale.' Snore Wife, who by this time is curiously aroused, stick her heads through the window. Anyway she bought one – which didn't help the trade gap at all. Little diggerydoo that it was parsened with deathly arsen, ickers. The woman (who was the wickered Queen in disgust) cackled away to her carstle in the hills larfing fit to bust.

Anyway the handsome Prince who was really Misst Cradock, found out and promptly ate the Wicked Queen and smashed up the mirror. After he had done this he journeyed to the house of the Several Dwarts and began to live with them. He refused to marry Snore Wife on account of his health, what with her being poissoned and that, but they came to an agreement much to the disgust of Sleepy – Grumpy – Sneeky – Dog – Smirkey – Alice? – Derick and Wimpy. The Dwarts clubbed together and didn't buy a new mirror, but always sang a happy song. They all livered happily ever aretor until they died – which somebody of them did naturally enough.

The Singu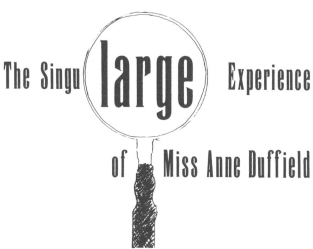large Experience of ✦ Miss Anne Duffield

I find it recornered in my nosebook that it was a dokey and winnie dave towart the end of Marge in the ear of our Loaf 1892 in Much Bladder, a city off the North Wold. Shamrock Womlbs had receeded a telephart whilst we sat at our lunch eating. He made no remark but the matter ran down his head, for he stud in front of the fire with a thoughtfowl face, smirking his pile, and casting an occasional gland at the massage. Quite sydney without warping he turd upod me with a miscarriage twinkle in his isle.

'Ellifitzgerrald my dear Whopper,' he grimmond then sharply 'Guess whom has broken out of jail Whopper?' My mind immediately recoughed all the caramels that had recently escaped or escaped from Wormy Scabs.

'Eric Morley?' I ventured. He shook his bed. 'Oxo Whitney?' I queered, he knotted in the infirmary. 'Rygo Hargraves?' I winston agreably.

'No, my dear Whopper, it's OXO WHITNEY' he bellowed as if I was in another room, and I wasn't.

'How d'you know Womlbs?' I whispered excretely.

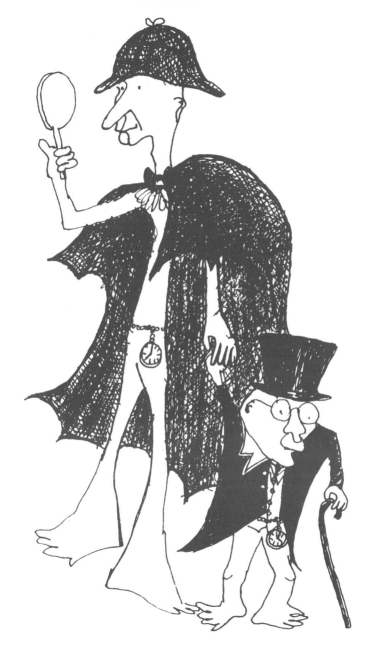

'Harrybellafonte, my dear Whopper.' At that precise morman a tall rather angularce tall thin man knocked on the door.
'By all accounts that must be he, Whopper.' I marvelled at his
acute osbert lancaster.

'How on urge do you know Womlbs' I asped, revealing my
bad armchair.

'Eliphantitus my deaf Whopper' he baggage knocking out
his pip on his large leather leg. In warped the favourite Oxo
Whitney none the worse for worms.

'I'm an escaped primrose Mr Womlbs' he grate darting
franetically about the room.

'Calm down Mr Whitney!' I interpolled 'or you'll have a
nervous breadvan.'

'You must be Doctored Whopper' he pharted. My friend
was starving at Whitney with a strange hook on his eager face,
that tightening of the lips, that quiver of the nostriches and
constapation of the heavy tufted brows which I knew so well.

'Gorra ciggie Oxo' said Womlbs quickly. I looked at my
colledge, hoping for some clue as to the reason for this sodden
outboard, he gave me no sign except a slight movement of his
good leg as he kicked Oxo Whitney to the floor. 'Gorra ciggie
Oxo' he reapeted almouth hysterically.

'What on urn are you doing my dear Womlbs' I imply; 'nay
I besiege you, stop lest you do this poor wretch an injury!'

'Shut yer face yer blubbering owld get' screamed Womlbs
like a man fermented, and laid into Mr Whitney something
powerful wat. This wasn't not the Shamrock Womlbs I used
to nose, I thought puzzled and hearn at this suddy change in
my old friend.

Mary Atkins pruned herselves in the mirrage, running her
hand wantanly through her large blond hair. Her tight dress

was cut low revealingly three or four blackheads, carefully scrubbed on her chess. She addled the final touches to her makeup and fixed her teeth firmly in her head. 'He's going to want me tonight' she thought and pictured his hamsome black curly face and jaundice. She looked at her clocks impatiently and went to the window, then leapt into her favorite armchurch, picking up the paper she glassed at the headlines. 'MORE NEGOES IN THE CONGO' it read, and there was, but it was the Stop Press which corked her eye. 'JACK THE NIPPLE STRIKE AGAIN.' She went cold all over, it was Sydnees and he'd left the door open.

'Hello lover' he said slapping her on the butter.

'Oh you did give me a start Sydnees' she shrieked laughing arf arfily.

'I always do my love' he replied jumping on all fours. She joined him and they galloffed quickly downstairs into a har- rased cab. 'Follow that calf' yelped Sydnees pointing a rude fingure.

'White hole mate!' said the scabbie.

'Why are we bellowing that card Sydnees?' inquired Mary fashionably.

'He might know where the party' explained Sydnees.

'Oh I see' said Mary looking up at him as if to say.

The journey parssed pleasantly enough with Sydnees and Mary pointing out places of interest to the scab driver; such as Buckinghell Parcel, the Horses of Parliamint, the Chasing of the Guards. One place of particularge interest was the Statue of Eric in Picanniny Surplass.

'They say that if you stand there long enough you'll meet a friend' said Sydnees knowingly, 'that's if your not run over.'

'God Save the Queens' shouted the scabbie as they passed the

Parcel for maybe the fourth time.

'Jack the Nipple' said Womlbs puffing deeply on his wife, 'is not only a vicious murderer but a sex meany of the lowest orgy.' Then my steamed collic relit his pig and walkered to the windy of his famous flat in Bugger St in London where it all hap‑pened. I pondled on his statemouth for a mormon then turding sharply I said. 'But how do you know Womlbs?'

'Alibabba my dead Whopper, I have seen the film' I knew him toby right for I had only read the comic.

That evenig we had an unexpeckled visitor, Inspectre Basil, I knew him by his tell‑tale unicorn.

'Ah Inspectre Basil mon cher amie' said Womlbs spotting him at once. 'What brings you to our humble rich establisment?'

'I come on behave of thousands' the Inspectre said sitting quietly on his operation.

'I feel I know why you are here Basil' said Womlbs eyeing he leg. 'It's about Jock the Cripple is it not?' The Inspectre smiled smiling.

'How did you guess?' I inquired all puzzle.

'Alecguiness my deep Whopper, the mud on the Inspectre's left, and also the buttock on his waistbox is misting.'

The Inspectre looked astoundagast and fidgeted nervously from one fat to the other. 'You neville sieze to amass me Mr Womlbs.'

'A drink genitalmen' I ventured, 'before we get down to the businose in hand in hand?' They both knotted in egremont and I went to the cocky cabinet. 'What would you prepare Basil, Bordom '83 or?'

'I'd rather have rather have rather' said the Inspectre who was a gourmless. After a drink and a few sam leeches Womlbs got up and paced the floor up and down up and down pacing.

'Why are you pacing the floor up and down up and down pacing dear Womlbs' I inquiet.

'I'm thinking alowed my deaf Whopper.' I looked over at the Inspectre and knew that he couldn't hear him either.

'Guess who's out of jail Mr Womlbs' the Inspectre said subbenly. Womlbs looked at me knowingly.

'Eric Morley?' I asked, they shook their heaths. 'Oxo Whitney?' I quart, again they shoot their heaps. 'Rygo Hargraves?' I wimpied.

'No my dear Whopper, OXO WHITNEY!' shouted Womlbs leaping to his foot. I looked at him admiring this great man all the morphia.

Meanwire in a ghasly lit street in Chelthea, a darkly clocked man with a fearful weapon, creeped about serging for revenge on the women of the streets for giving him the dreadfoot V.D. (Valentine Dyall). 'I'll kill them all womb by womb' he muffled between scenes. He was like a black shadow or negro on that dumb foggy night as he furtively looked for his neck victim. His minds wandered back to his childhook, remembering a vague thing or two like his mother and farmer and how they had beaten him for eating his sister. 'I'm demented' he said checking his dictionary, 'I should bean at home on a knife like these.' He turned into a dim darky and spotted a light.

Mary Atkins pruned herselves in the mirrage running her hand wantanly through her large blond hair. Her tight dress was cut low revealingly three or four *more* blackheads carefully scrubbed on her chess. Business had been bad lately and what with the cost of limping. She hurriedly tucked in her gooseberries and opened the door. 'No wonder business is bad' she remarked as she caught size of her hump in the hall mirror.

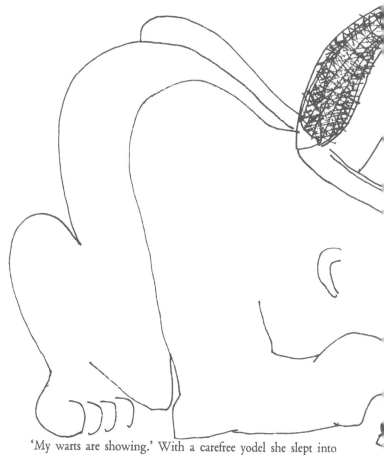

'My warts are showing.' With a carefree yodel she slept into the street and caught a cab to her happy humping grounds. 'That Sydnees's nothing but a pimple living on me thus' she thought 'lazing about day in day off, and here's me plowing my train up and down like Soft Arthur and you know how soft Arthur.' She got off as uterus at Nats Café and took up her

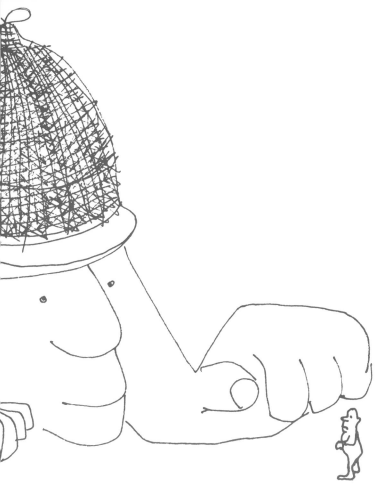

position. 'They'll never even see me in this fog' she muttered switching on her lamps. Just then a blasted Policemat walked by. 'Blasted Policemat' she shouted, but luckily he was deaf. 'Blasted deaf Policemat' she shouted. 'Why don't yer gerra job!'

Little did she gnome that the infamous Jack the Nipple was

only a few street away. 'I hope that blasted Jack the Nipple isn't only a few streets away,' she said, 'he's not right in the heads.'

'How much lady' a voice shocked her from the doorways of Nats. Lucky for him there was a sale on so they soon retched an agreament. A very high class genderman she thought as they walked quickly together down the now famous Carringto Average.

'I tell yer she whore a good woman Mr Womlbs sir' said Sydnees Aspinall.

'I quite believe you Mr Asterpoll, after all you knew her better than me and dear old buddy friend Whopper, but we are not here to discuss her merits good or otherwives, we are here, Mr Asronaute, to discover as much information as we can about the unfortunate and untidy death of Mary Atkins.' Womlbs looked the man in the face effortlessly.

'The name's Aspinall guvnor' said the wretched man.

'I'm deleware of your name Mr Astracan.' Womlbs said looking as if he was going to smash him.

'Well as long as you know,' said Aspinall wishing he'd gone to Safely Safely Sunday Trip. Womlbs took down the entrails from Aspinall as quickly as he could, I could see that they weren't on the same waveleg.

'The thing that puddles me Womlbs,' I said when we were alone, 'is what happened to Oxo Whitney?' Womlbs looged at me intently, I could see that great mind was thinking as his tufted eyepencil knit toboggen, his strong jew jutted out, his nosepack flared, and the limes on his fourheads wrinkled.

'That's a question Whopper.' he said and I marveled at his grammer. Next day Womlbs was up at the crack of dorchester, he didn't evening look at the moaning papers. As yewtree I fixed his breakfast of bogard, a gottle of geer, a slice of jewish bread, three eggs with little liars on, two rashes of bacon, a bowel of Rice Krustchovs, a fresh grapeful, mushrudes, some freed tomorrows, a basket of fruits, and a cup of teens.

'Breakfeet are ready' I showbody 'It's on the table.' But to my supplies he'd already gone. 'Blast the wicker basket yer grannie sleeps in.' I thought 'Only kidding Shamrock' I said remembering his habit of hiding in the cupboard.

That day was an anxious one for me as I waited for news of my dear friend, I became fretful and couldn't finish my Kenno-meat, it wasn't like Shamrock to leave me here all by my own, lonely; without him I was at large. I rang up a few close itamate friends but they didn't know either, even Inspectre Basil didn't know, and if anybody should know, Inspectre Basil should 'cause he's a Police. I was a week lately when I saw him again and I was shocked by his apeerless, he was a dishovelled rock. 'My God Womlbs' I cried 'My God, what on earth have you been?'

'All in good time Whopper' he trousered. 'Wait till I get my breast back.'

I poked the fire and warmed his kippers, when he had mini-coopered he told me a story which to this day I can't remember.

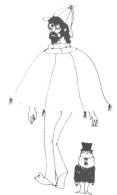

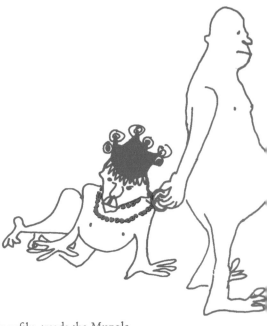

Softly softly, treads the Mungle
Thinner thorn behaviour street.
Whorg canteell whorth bee asbin?
Cam we so all complete,
With all our faulty bagnose?

The Mungle pilgriffs far awoy
Religeorge too thee worled.
Sam fells on the waysock-side
And somforbe on a gurled,
With all her faulty bagnose!

The Faul

108

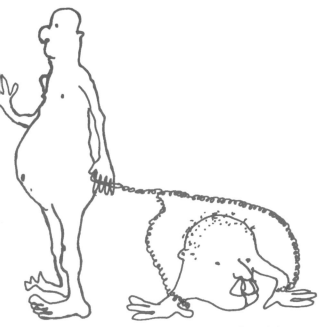

gnose

Our Mungle speaks tonife at eight
He tell us wop to doo
And bless us cotten sods again
Oamnipple to our jew
(With all their faulty bagnose).

Bless our gurlished wramfeed
Me curséd café kname
And bless thee loaf he eating
With he golden teeth aflame
Give us OUR faulty bagnose!

Good Mungle blaith our meathalls
Woof mebble morn so green the wheel
Staggaboon undie some grapeload
To get a little feel
of my own faulty bagnose.

Its not OUR faulty bagnose now
Full lust and dirty hand
Whitehall the treble Mungle speak
We might as wealth be band
Including your faulty bagnose

Give us thisbe our daily tit
Good Mungle on yer travelled
A goat of many coloureds
Wiberneth all beneath unravelled
And not so MUCH OF YER FAULTY BAGNOSE!

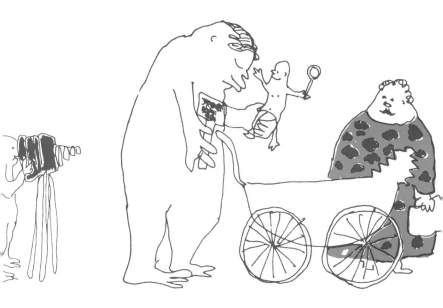

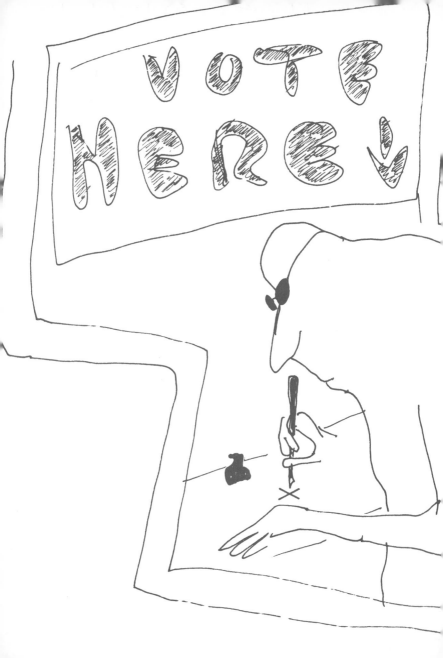

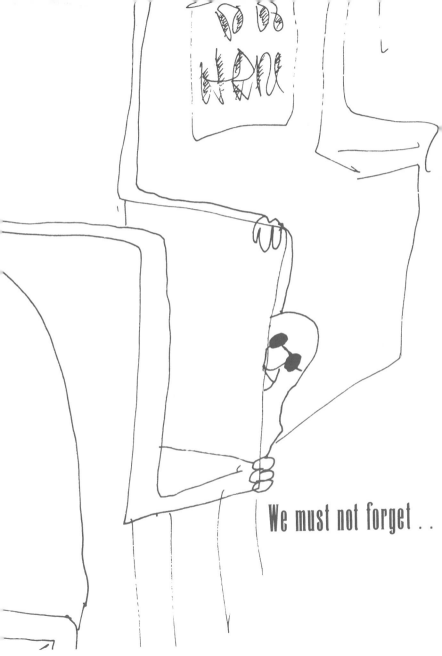

We must not forget . .

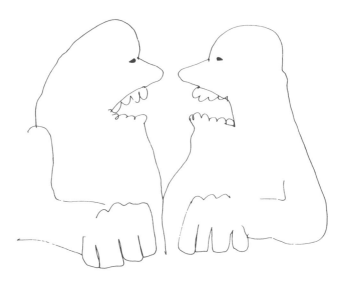

Azue orl gnome, Harassed Wilsod won the General Erection, with a very small marjorie over the Torchies. Thus pudding the Laboring Partly back into powell after a large abcess. This he could not have done withoutspan the barking of thee Trade Onions, heady by Frenk Cunnings (who noun has a SAFE SEAT in Nuneating thank you and Fronk (only 62) Bowels hasn't).

Sir Alice Doubtless-Whom was – quote – 'bitherly ditha-pointed' but managed to keep smirking on his 500,000 acre estate in Scotland with a bit of fishing and that.

The Torchies (now in apperition) have still the capable

...the General Erection

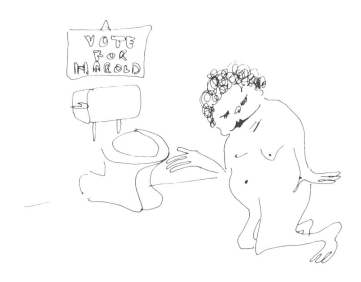

qualities of such disable men as Rabbit Bunloaf and the very late Harrods McMillion. What, you arsk, happened to Answerme Enos (ex Prim Minicar) after that Suez pudding, peaple are saying. Well I don't know.

We must not forget the great roles played out by Huge Foot and Dingie in capturing a vote or tomb. We must not forget Mrs Wilsod showing her toilets on telly. We must not forget Mr Caravans loving smile on Budgie Day as he raised the price of the Old Age Pests. We must not forget Mr Caravans lovely smile when he raised the price of the M.P.s (Mentals of Parliament) wagers as well also. We must not forget Joke Grimmace (LIB). We must not forget to issue clogs to all the G.P. Ostmen who are foing great things somewhere and also we must not forget to Post Early for Christsake.

Lastly but not priest, we must not forget to put the clocks back when we all get bombed. Harold.

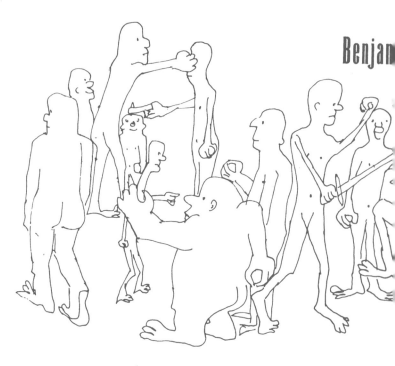

Benjaman halted his grave flow of speach and lug off a cigarf he knew where peeky boon! He wretched overy and berlin all the tootsdes.

'It were all nok a limpcheese then a work ferce bottle. Ai warp a grale regrowth on, withy boorly replenishamatsaty troop, and harlas a wedreally to fight. We're save King of pampices when all the worm here me aid.' I inadvertabably an unobtrusive neyber had looke round and seen a lot of goings off, you know how they are. Anywart, I say get a battlyard pussload, ye scurry navvy, I beseige of all my bogglephart, way with his kind farleny and grevey cawlers. But Benjaman was a rather

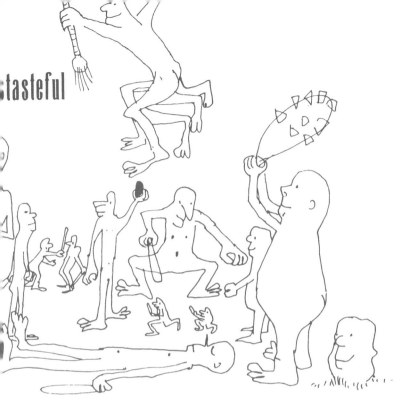

man for all I cared. I eyed he looking, 'Ben' I cried 'You are rather man.' He looked at me hardly with a brown trowel. 'I know' he said, 'but I do a steady thirsty.' I were overwhelped with heem grate knowaldge, you darn't offer mead and monk with all these nobody, I thought. A man like he shall haff all the bodgy poodles in his hands. 'Curse ye baldy butters, and Ai think its a pritty poreshow when somebottle of my statue has to place yongslave on my deposite.'

'Why – why?' I cribble all tawdry in my best sydneys.

To this day I'll never know.

THE END

The Wumberlog (or The Magic Dog)

Whilst all the tow was sleepy
Crept a little boy from bed
To fained the wondrous peoble
Wot lived when they were dead.

He packed a little voucher
For his dinner 'neath a tree.
'Perhumps a tiny dwarf or two
Would share abite with me?

'Perchamp I'll see the Wumberlog
The highly feathered crow,
The larfing leaping Harristweed
And good old Uncle Joe.'

He packed he very trunkase,
Clean sockers for a week,
His book and denzil for his notes,
Then out the windy creep.

He met him friendly magic dog,
All black and curlew too,
Wot flew him fast in second class
To do wot he must do.

'I'll leave you now sir,' said the dog,
'But just before I go
I must advise you,' said his friend
'This boat to careflee row.'

'I thank you kindly friendly pal,
I will,' and so he did,
And floated down towards the land
Where all the secrets hid.

What larfs aplenty did he larf,
It seeming so absurd;
Whilst losing all his oars,
On his head he found a bird.

'Hello,' the bird said, larfing too,
'I hope you don't mind me,
I've come to guide you here on in,
In case you're lost at sea.'

Well fancy that, the boy thought,
I never knew till now
That birds could speak so plainly.
He wondered – wonder how?

'What kind of bird are you sir?'
He said with due respect,
'I hope I'm not too nosey
But I didn't not expect.'

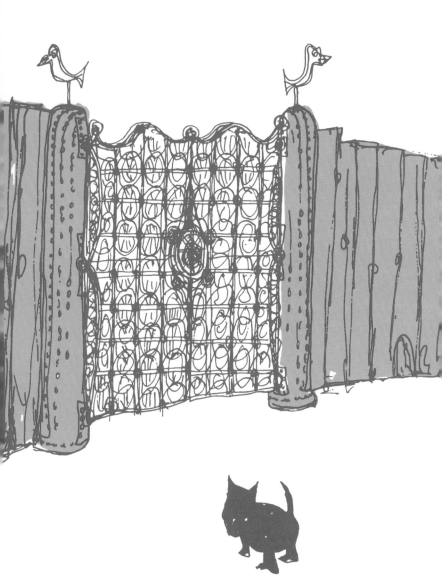

'I am a wumberlog you see,'
The bird replied – all coy,
'The highly feathered species lad,
You ought to jump for joy.'

'I would I would, if only, but
You see – well – yes, oh dear,
The thing is dear old Wumberlog
I'm petrefried with fear!'

'Now don't be silly' said the bird,
'I friendly – always – and
I'm not like Thorpy Grumphlap,
I'll show you when we land.'

And soon the land came interview,
A 'tastic sight for sure,
An island with an eye to see
To guide you into shore.

'Hard to starboard' said a tree,
'Yer focsle mainsle blast
Shivver timbers wayard wind
At last yer've come at last.'

'You weren't expecting me, I hope'
The boy said, puzzled now.
'Of course we are' a thing said,
Looking slightly like a cow.

'We've got the kettle going lad,'
A cheerful apple say,
'I'll bring a bag of friends along
Wot you can have for tay.'

A teawell ate, with dog and tree
Is not a common sight,
Especially when the dog himself
Had started off the flight.

'How did you get here curlew friend?'
The boy said all a maze.
'The same way you did, in a boat,'
The dog yelled through the haze.

'Where are all the peoble, please,
Wot live when they are dead?
I'd like to see them if I may
Before I'm back in bed.'

'You'll see them son,' a carrot said,
'Don't hurry us; you know
You've got to eat a plate of me
Before we let you go!'

Then off to see the peoble whom
The lad had come to see
And in the distance there he saw
A group of twelve or three.

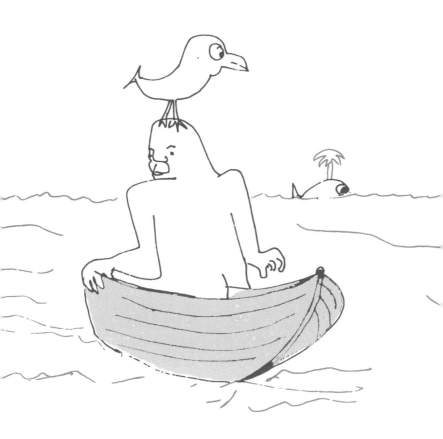

A little further on at last
There were a lot or more,
All digging in the ground and that,
All digging in the floor.

'What are you digging all the time?'
He asked them like a brother.
Before they answered he could see
They really dug each other.

In fact they took it turns apiece
To lay down in the ground
And shove the soil upon the heads
Of all their friends around.

Well, what a sight! I ask you now.
He had to larf out loud.
Before he knew what happened
He'd gathered quite a crowed.

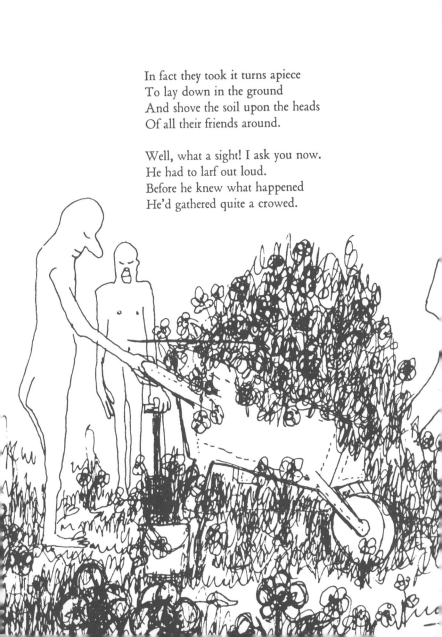

Without a word, and spades on high,
They all dug deep and low,
And placed the boy into a hole
Next to his Uncle Joe.

'I told you not to come out here,'
His uncle said, all sad.
'I had to Uncle,' said the boy.'
'You're all the friend I had.'

With just their heads above the ground
They bade a fond goodbye,
With all the people shouting out
'Heres mud into your eye!'
(And there certainly was.)

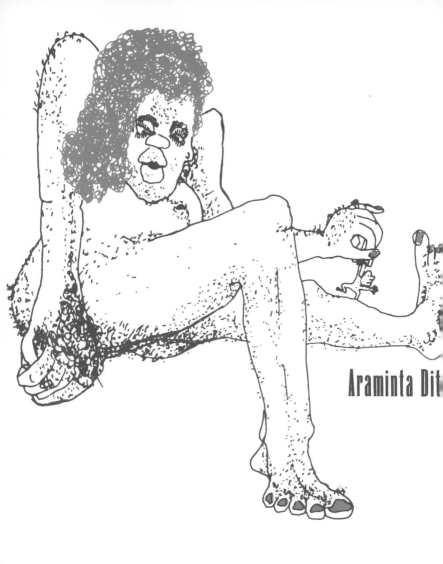

Araminta Dit

Araminta Ditch was always larfing. She woof larf at these, larf at thas. Always larfing she was. Many body peofle woof look atat her saying, 'Why does that Araminta Ditch keep larfing?' They could never understamp why she was ever larfing about the place. 'I hope she's not at all larfing at me,' some peokle would say, 'I certainly hope that Araminta Ditch is not larfing at me.'

One date Araminta rose up out of her duffle bed, larfing as usual with that insage larf peojle had come to know her form.

'Hee! hee! hee!' She larfed all the way down to breakfart.

'Hee! hee! hee!' She gurgled over the morman papiers.

'Hee! hee! hee!' Continude Araminta on the buzz to wirk.

This pubbled the passages and condoctor equally both. 'Why is that boot larfing all the time?' Inqueered an elderberry passengeorge who trabelled regularge on that roof and had a write to know.

'I bet nobody knows why I am always larfing.' Said Ara-minta to herself privately, to herself. 'They would dearly love to know why I am always larfing like this to myselve privately to myselve. I bet some peoble would really like to know.' She was right, off course, lots of peotle would.

Araminta Ditch had a boyfred who could never see the joke. 'As long as she's happy,' he said. He was a good man. 'Pray tell me, Araminta, why is it that you larf so readily. Yeaye, but I am sorly troubled sometimes when thy larfter causes sitch tribulation and embarresment amongst my family and elders.' Araminta would larf all the more at an outburp like this, even to the point of hysteriffs. 'Hee! hee! hee!' She would scream as if possesed by the very double himself.

'That Araminta Ditch will have to storp orl these larfing; she will definitely have to storp it. I will go crazy if she don't storp it.' This was the large voice of her goodly neighbore, Mrs Cramsby, who lived right next door and looked after the cats whilst Araminta was at work. 'Takes a good deal of looking after these cat when she's at work – and that's nothing to larf about!'

The whole street had beginning to worry about Araminta's larfter. Why? hadn't she been larfing and living there for nye-bevan thirty years, continually larfing hee! hee! and annoying them? They began to hold meters to see what could be done – after all they had to live with her hadn't they? It was them who had to always keep hearing her inane larftor. At one such meetinge they deciple to call on the help of Aramintas' boy-fiend who was called Richard (sometimes Richard the Turd, but thats another story). 'Well I dont know dear friends,' said Richard, who hated them all. This was at the second meetink!

Obvouslieg samting hed tow be doon – and quickly.

Aramintas' face was spreading aboon the country, peochle fram all walks of leg began to regarden her with a certain insight left.

'What canon I do that would quell this mirth what is gradually drying me to drink, have I not bespoken to her often, betting her to cease, threatling – cajolson – arsking, pleases stop this larftor Araminta. I am at the end of my leather – my cup kenneth conner,' Richard say. The people of the street mubbered in agreement, what could he do? He was foing his vest. 'We will ask the Vicar,' said Mrs Crambsey, 'Surely he can exercise it out of her?' The peodle agreed – 'Surely the Vicar can do it if anybotty can.' The Vicar smiled a funny little smile wholst the goo people splained the troumer. When they had had finished speaching he rose up grandly from his barthchair and said loud and clear 'What do you mean exactly?' The peodle sighed an slowlies started to start again telling him about the awful case of Araminta's larfing.

'You mean she just keeps larfing fer no a parent season?' he said brightly. 'Yess that's it fazackerly Vicar,' said Richard, 'morning noon and nige, always larfing like a mad thin.' The Vicar looked up from his knitting and opened his mouths.

'Something will have to be done about that girl larfing all the time. It's not right.'

'I really doughnut see that it is any concervative of thiers whether i larf or nament,' sighed Araminta over a lengthy victim. 'The trifle with the peomle around here is that they have forgoden how, I repeat, how to larf, reverend, that's what I think anyhow.'

She was of corset talking to the extremely reverend LIONEL HUGHES. She had gone to see him in case he could help her in any small way, considering he was always spouting off about helping peouple she thought she'd give him a try as it were. 'What can I say my dear, I mean what can I say?' Araminta looked at the holy fink with disbelief. 'What do you mean – what can I say – don't ask me what to say. I cam here to ask you for help and you have the audacidacidity to ask me what to say – is that all you have to say?' she yellowed. 'I know exactly how you feel Samantha, I had a cousin the same way, couldn't see a thin   without his glasgows.'

Araminta stood up in a kind of suit, she picked up her own mongels and ran seriously out of the room. 'No wonder he only gets three in on Sunday!' she exclaimed to a small group of wellwishers.

A year or more passedover with no changei in Araminta's strange larfing. 'Hee! hee! hee!' she went drivan herself and everone around her insane. THERE SEEMED NO END TO THE PROBLEM. This went on for eighty years until Araminta died larfing. This did not help her neighbors much. They had all died first, – which was one of the many things that Araminta died larfing off.

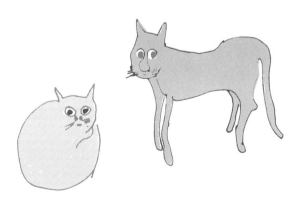

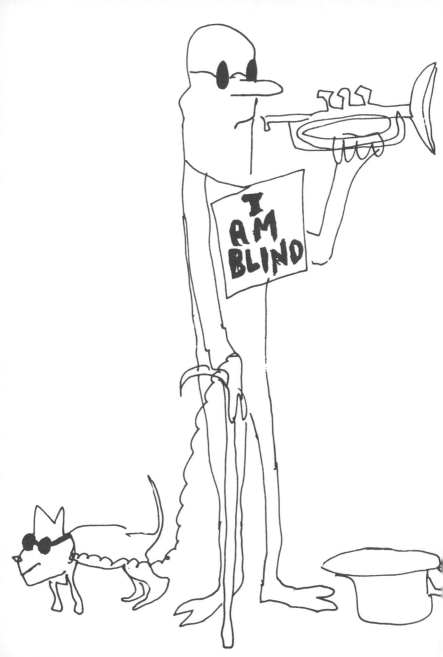

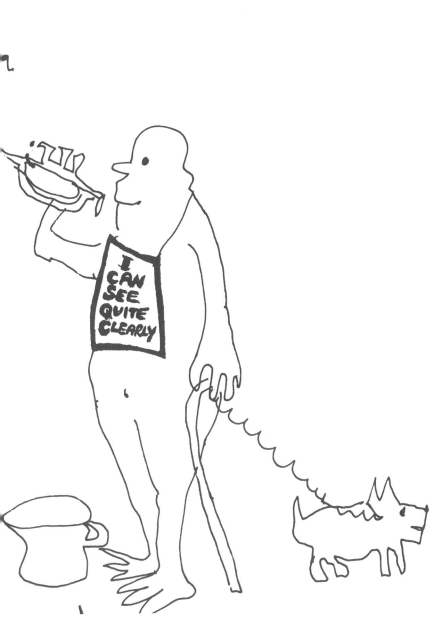

CASSANDLE

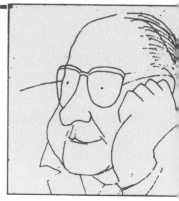

‘ Mike (*Round the Worst
in A Tall Canoe, the late*)
Toddy would have liked me. ’

You all know me

How many times have I warned you all about my telephone? Well it happened again! *Once more I couldn't get through to my Aunty Besst, and yet again I nearly didn't get my famous column with a picture of me inset through those damn blasted operators!* YOU know how I hate those damn blasted operators. You all know me. THIRTY TWO times I tried to get through with my famous column and thirty two times I was told to 'Gerroff the line yer borein' owld gassbag!' When I told a colleague or two, they couldn't not believe it, after all hadn't I been writing the same thing for sixty years? You all know me . . .

The way I see it

How many moron of these incredible sleasy backward, bad, deaf monkeys, parsing as entertainers, with thier FLOPTOPPED hair, falling about the place like Mary PICKFORD, do I have to put up with? *The* way I see it, a good smell in the Army would cure them, get rid of a few more capitalist barskets (OOPS!). Not being able to stand capitalism, I fail to see why those awful common lads make all that money, in spite of me and the government in a society such as ours where our talent will out.

I know I'm a bald old get with glasses (SEE PICTURE). *Maybe I ought to be thankfull, but I doubt it . . .*

Koms der revolution

Caviar is collected for me with ▌lywood. Do you remember whe▌ had dinner with that super spif▌ showdog Mike 9 (Round the Wal▌ Eighty Days, the late) Toddy? V▌ he loved caviarse/great pots of ▌ and he assulmed derry boddy elf ▌ and if they didn't, they should, da▌ it (OPPS!). *You* all know me, we▌ don't like it, and I find myself (s▌ times) fighting a fierce and won▌ full verbal battle as to whethe▌ should be fòrthed against *my* ▌ to eat this *costly* delicasy from ▌ Caspian Sea. Quite orften I l▌ but thats Socialism. (*You know m*▌

Mike (*Round the Worst in A Tall Ca*▌ *the late*) *Toddy would have liked me.*▌

I suppose a lot of you have never ▌ the chance of refusing this cos▌ delicacy, believe me fans, you ne▌ will if we keep building all th▌ bombs . . .

Until tomorrow friends when I (Y▌ ALL KNOW ME) will be back w▌ the same picture, but a DIFFERE▌ QUOTE brothers.

Good Day, (The way I see it!)

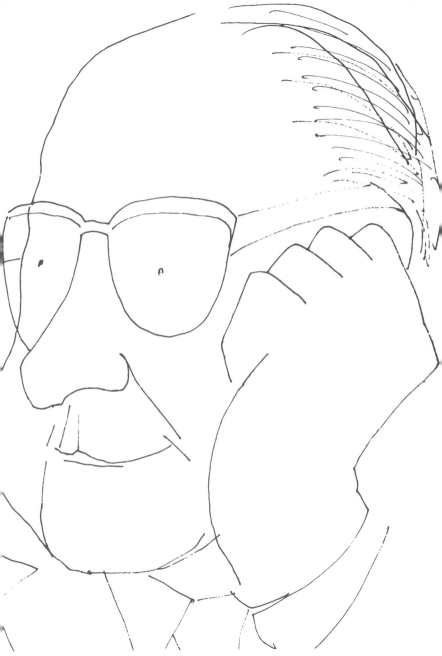

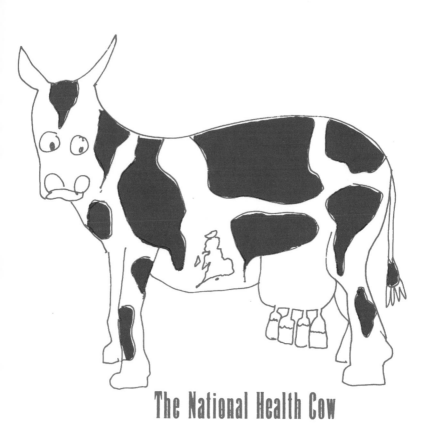

The National Health Cow

I strolled into a farmyard
When no-one was about
Treading past the troubles
I raised my head to shout.

'Come out the Cow with glasses,'
I called and rolled my eye.
It ambled up toward me,
I milked it with a sigh.

'You're just in time' the cow said,
Its eyes were all aglaze,
'I'm feeling like an elephant,
I aren't been milked for days.'

'Why is this?' I asked it,
Tugging at its throttles.
'I don't know why, perhaps it's 'cause
MY milk comes out in bottles.'

'That's handy for the government,'
I thought, and in a tick
The cow fell dead all sudden
(*I'd smashed it with a brick*).

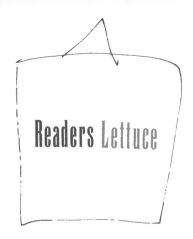

Readers Lettuce

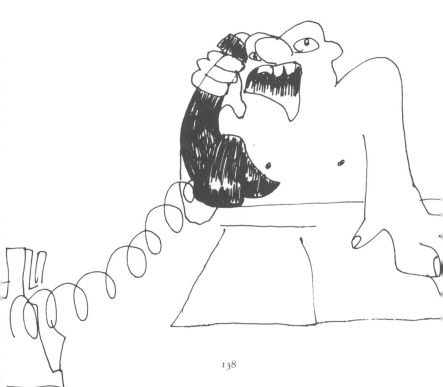

Dear Sir,

IF Mr Mothballs (Feb, 23 Sun'Taimes, page 8. col 4),
thinks that the Hon gentleman (Norman Ccough). Well I'm
here to tell him (Mr Mothballs) that he has bitten off more
than he can chew. How dearie imply that Mr Ccough is
socially inpurdent? Was it not Ccough whom started off the
worled wide organiseationses, which in turn brought imidiate
response from the Western Alliance (T.U.R.). If Mr Smith-
barbs sincerely imagines that Indonegro is really going to
attack the Australian continent with the eyes of the worled
upon them I can only asulme that he (Mr Smallburns) has
taken leaf of his sentries! Has he forgetting Mr Ccough's
graet speek at the Asembly of Natives? Is he also forbett-
ing that hithertoe unpressydessy charter- the Blested Old
Widows - which was carried through the House with a Majollity
vote?

In future I hobe thet Mr Smellbarth will refrian
frog makeing wild and dangeroo statemonths.

Iremain still,

yours for the arsking,

Jennifarse Cough (no relations).

P.S. CAN I HEVE A PHOTY OF WINDY STANDSTILL?

Editors Football.

Well maa'mm, the old Coblers think you're a very plucky
christion. Wish there were a few more like yourself maa'mm!!!!

Silly Norman

'I really don't know woot tow mak of these.' said Norman, as he sorted through him Chrimbas posed. 'It seem woot I git mower litters und parskels than woot I know peoples, it suplizeses moi moor et moor each yar, as moor on these pareskle keep cooming. I really doon't knaw whew all they body are – seddling ik all this.' He clab quitely too the fire, sheving a few mough ruddish awn. 'It's came tow a pretty parse when I don't evil knew where they cam frog.' Norman coop an stetty keel and prumptly wed intow thee kitcheon tow put up thee kettle

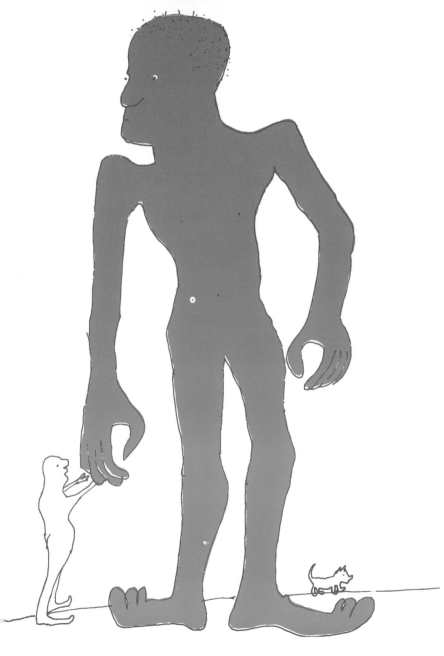

orn. 'I might as welsh mak me a cooper tea, I night as welp hev a chocolush birskit as well, wile I do noddy.' So saying so he marshed offer to that teapod and tap it to that sing: bud to he grey suffise – what! – bat noo warty. 'Goob heralds! what's all of thiz goinge awn? Doe mein ice desleeve me? Am I knot loofing at me owen sing-unice, and there be know warty?' He was quait raight, lo! the warty didn noo apear, trey as he maybe.

Off course we all know whey this warty do no coomb, becourgh the tangs they are awl freezup, awl on they, awl they freezop. Norman dig knort know that, for Norman him a silly man – yes – Norman is sorft. 'OH deally meat! oh woe isme, wart canada, ther are nay werters toe mick a caper tay, ange me moover she arther cooming ferty too. I shall heave two gough nextador, perhats they might hall hefty.' Sow Norman he gentry poots his had hand coat orn makeing sewer to wrave hisself op like he moomy tell him, broosh beyond the ears and out of that frant door he ghost. To him truly amasemaid, he fainds nought a houfe nought a hough inside! Wart on earth is heffer-ing? – why – there iznot a hug tobeseen, not anyway fer miles aboot. 'Goody Griff, which artery in HEFFER harold be thy norm! is these not thet enid of the worm? Surely to goosestep I am nit that larst man on earn?' he fell suddy to the ground weefy and whaley crizeling tuber Lawn aboove to savfre him or judge spare a friend or to. 'I wilf give of awl my wordy posesions, awl me foren stabs, awl me classicow rechords, awl me fave rave pidgeons of Humpty Littlesod thee great nothing. All these oh wondrouse Sailor up above, I offer ye if only yer will save me!'

Normans mather, who you remembrane, was a combing tooty, was shorked when she cam acroose him lyinge awn the floor thus crying. 'My dear NORMAN!' she screege, 'Wart in Griffs' nave are you doing, why are you carroling on this way?' She wogged slightly over to her own son, with a woddied loof in her eye. 'Police don't garryon like this my son, tell Muddle werts the metre.' Norman raved himself slowly and sabbly locked at her. 'Carrot you see, mubber, Griff have end the worled. I only went to guess sam warty, and then it dibble wirk, so I went to go necktie to a nebough and I saw wit had happened – GRIFF had ended the worl. I saw nothing – every where there where no neybers. Oh Mather wet is hap⁄pening?' Normans mither take won loog at he with a disabe⁄leafed spression on her head. 'My Golf! Norman wit are yuo torking about turn? Donald you member thet there have been nobodys livfing here ever? Rememble whensday first move in how you say – "Thank Heavy there are no peoplre about this place, I want to be aloef?" have you fergit all thistle?' Norman lucked op at he mam (stikl cryling) with teeth in his eye, saying – 'Muther, thou art the one, the power ov atterny, for heavan sakes amen. Thank you dear mether, I had truly forgot. I am a silly Norman!' They booth link arbs and walk brightly to the house.

'Fancy me ferbetting that no⁄bottle lives roynd here mother! Fantasie forgetting thet!' They each laff together as they head four the kitchenn – and lo! – that warty runs again, the sunbeefs had done it, and they booth have tea, booth on them. Which jub shaw yer – –

> 'However blackpool tower maybe,
> In time they'll bassaway.
> Have faith and trumpand B B C –
> Griffs' light make bright your day.'
>
> AMEN (and mickaela dentist.)

Mr. Boris Morris

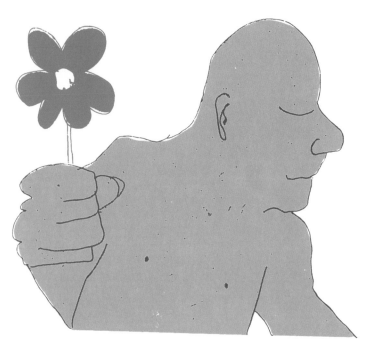

However Mr Boris Morris was morgan thankful for his narrow escape is largely put down to his happy knack of being in the right place at the right place. For stance, Boris was the one whom cornered Miss Pearl Staines at her impromtu but lighthearted garbage partly.

'Miss Staines' he had shouted 'how come you never invited yer sister to the do?'

'For the same reason I didn't invite you Mr Morris' she replight reaching for anoven helping.

Boris was no fudge, he quickly melted into the backcloth like an old cake, slighly taking candy shots of Miss Staines with her relatively.

'She won't invite me to the next do either' he remarked out loud with above average clarity.

Boris was elsie the man whom got the photies of the Dupe of Bedpan doing things at the anyearly jap festival, much to the supper of the Duchess set. Thus then was Boris Morris a man of great reknown and familiarity, accepted at do's of the wealthy and the poor alike hell. He was knew as the jew with a view, and he had. Not long after one of his more well known escapades, he was unfortunable to recieve a terrible blow to his ego. He was shot in the face at a Hunt Ball but nobody peaple found out till the end becaugh they all thought it was a clever mask.

'What a clever mask that man has on,' was heard once or twig.

It was not the end of Boris as you might well imargin, but even before his face set he was to easily recognizable at most places, with peaple pointing at him saying thing like 'What a good shot' and other. All this set Boris thinking, specially in the morning when he was shaving his scabs, as only he knew how.

'Must fix this blob of mine' he'd smile over a faceful of blotting paper.

'You certainly must dear' said his amiable old wife, 'what with me not getting any younger.'

Bernice's Sheep

This night I lable down to sleep
With hefty heart and much saddened
With all the bubbles of the world
Bratting my boulders
Oh dear sheep

I slapter counting one be one
Till I can cow nomore this day
Till bethny hard aches leave we
Elbing my ethbreeds
Dear Griff's son

What keeps me alberts owl felloon
That is earl I ask from anybottly
That I grape me daily work
Cronching our batter
My own bassoon.

Can I get a gribble of me
Should I heffer alway sickened
Should you nabbie my furbern
Wilfing their busbie
Oh dear me.

No! I shall streze my eber⁄teap!
With lightly loaf and great larfter
With head held eye and all
Graffing my rhimber
Oh dear sheep.

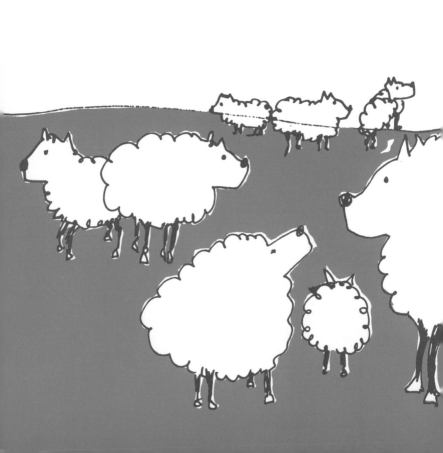

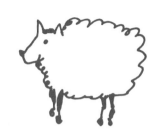
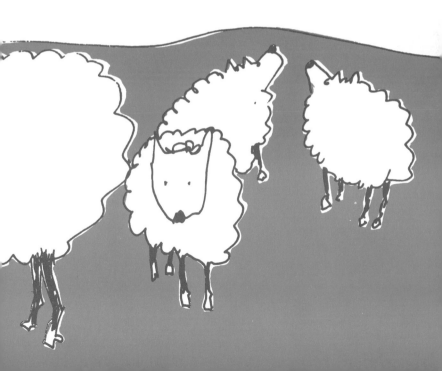

Last Will and Testicle

'I, Barrold Reginald Bunker-Harquart
being of sound mind you, limp and bodie,
do on this day the 18 of Septemper 1924th,
leave all my belodgings estate and brown
suits to my nice neice Elsie. The above
afformentioned hereafter to be kept in a
large box untit she is 21 of age, then to be
released amongst a birthdave party given
in her honour. She will then be wheeled
gladly into the Great Hall or kitchen,
and all my worldly good heaped upon her
in abundance. Thus accordian to my word
will this be carried out as I lie in the
ground getting eaten.'

This then was the last will and testicle of I Barrold Reginald Bunker-Harquart, which was to change the lives of so many peoble – speciality little Elsie whom was only thirteens.

'Are you sure I have to stay in the box?' asked Elsie childishly.

'Yer not deaf are yer?' yelled Freud Q.C. what was helping. 'Yer 'eard the familias solister as good as we didn't yer?'

'I was only makeing conversation' replied Elisie who was only thirteen.

Just then Elisies dear Old Nanny Harriette broke down in tears and everybody walked quietly out of the room leaving her to her grease, except Dr (not the) Barnado.

'There there Harriette, that won't bring the Mastered back' he said knowingly.

'I know I know' she bluttered 'its not that, its where are we going to find a box to fit *her* foot? tell me that, where are we going to find a box to fit *her* foot?' Luckily the Dr knew a carpentor in the village who was A WONDER WITH WOOD. 'I'm a wonder with wood.' he used to say, as he sored his way through life – with a nail in one hand and polio in the other (his light hand being stronger than his lest). 'Children should be seized and not hard' was something Uncle Barrold had always said and *even* Old Nanny had always replied 'Overy clown has a silver lifeboat' which always dried him ap.

Anywait, Elisie was soon entombed in her made to marion box, and people from miles adavies would come and visit HER, but only when it was sunny – for she was kept rightly in the garden. 'At least she'll get some fresh air.' argued Old Nanny – and she was right.

Three years parst and a great change had come over Elsie.

Her once lovely skin was now roof and ready, some say it was that last bitter winter, others say it wasn't. Her warm smile which made one forget her hairlip was now a sickly grin, but enough of that.

Less and lessless people came to visit Elsie especially since Old Nanny had put the price up. The Dr had kindly devised a scheme whereby Elsie could call for anything she wanted. It was a primitive affair, but effective – just a simple microphone tied into Elsie's mouth. This was attached to a louder speaker in the kitchen. Of course when Old Nanny was away on holiday, she would turn the speaker off. 'No point in her shouting if I'm away' she would explain.

The years flew by for Elsie in her own box, sooner no than it was coming round to her twenty/first burly. 'I hope I get the key of the door' she thought, forgetting for a moment she was getting the whole house. The place was was certainly in a state of anticipatient on the ear of Elsie's birthdaft, and Old Nanny celebrated by bringing her into the house for 'a warm by the fire' as she put it. Unfortunately Old Nanny seemed to place birthday Elsie too near the big old fireplace and her box caught alight with Elsie still wrapped firmly inside like her Uncle asked.

'She didn't even eat her cake,' said Old Nanny tearfulham to Dr (not the) Bernardo the next morning.

'Never mind' he wryled. 'we'll give it the dog, he'll eat anything.'

With that the Dr leaped over and gave Old Nanny a thorough examination on her brand new carpet.

'You can't have your cake and eat it' said a cheerful paying guessed adding, 'Statistics state that 90% of more accidents are caused by burning children in the house.'

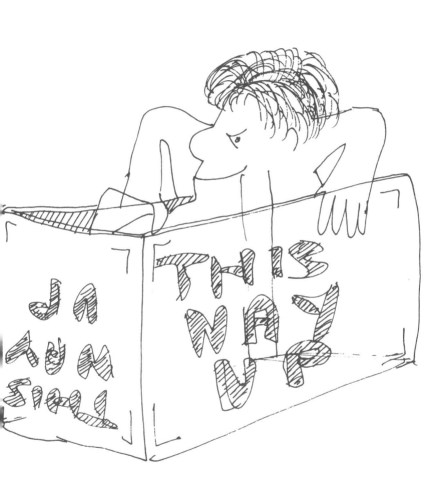

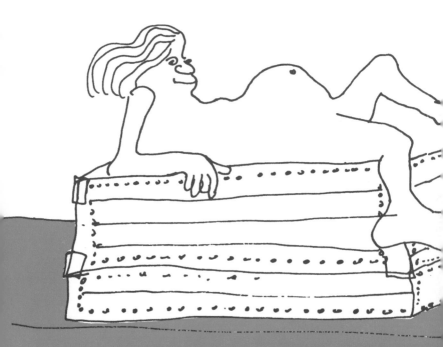

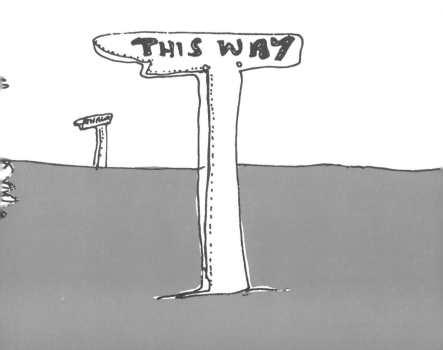

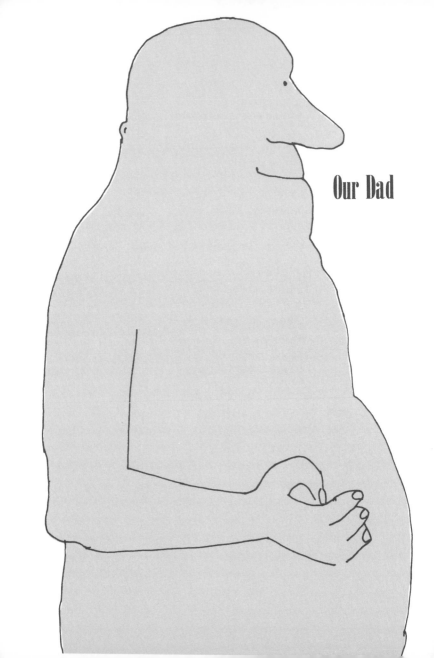

Our Dad

It wasn't long before old dad
Was cumbersome – a drag.
He seemed to get the message and
Began to pack his bag.

'You don't want me around,' he said,
'I'm old and crippled too.'
We didn't have the heart to say
'You're bloody right it's true.'

He really took an age and more
To pack his tatty kleid.
We started coughing by the door,
To hurry him outside.

'I'm no use to man nor beast,'
He said, his eye all wet.
'That's why we're getting rid of you,
Yer stupid bastard, get.'

His wrinkled face turned up to us
A pleading in his look;
We gave him half-a-crown apiece
And polished up his hook.

'Its not that we don't like you dad.'
Our eyes were downcast down.
'We've tried to make a go of it
Yer shrivelled little clown!'

At last he finished packing all,
His iron hand as well.
He even packed the penis
What he'd won at bagatell.

''Spect you'll write a line or two?'
He whined – who could resist?
We held his face beneath the light
And wrote a shopping list.

'Goodbye my sons and fare thee well,
I blame yer not yer see,
It's all yer mothers doing lads,
She's had it in for me.'

'You leave our mother out of this!'
We screamed all fury rage,
'At least she's working for her keep
And nearly twice your age!'

'I'd sooner starve than be a whore!'
The old man said, all hurt.
'Immoral earnings aren't for me,
and living off her dirt.'

'She washes everyday,' we said
Together, all at once.
'It's more than can be said for you
Yer dirty little ponce!'

At last upon the doorstep front
He turned and with a wave
He wished us all 'Good Heavens'
And hoped we'd all behave.

'The best of luck to you old dad!'
We said with slight remorse,
'You'll dig it in the workhouse man.'
(He wouldn't though of course.)

'Ah well he's gone and thats a fact,'
We muttered after lunch,
And hurried to the room in which
He used to wash his hunch.

'Well here's a blessing in disguise;
Not only money too;
He's left his pension book as well
The slimy little jew!'

'What luck we'll have a party
Inviting all our friend.
We've only one but she's a laugh
She lets us all attend.'

We never heard from dad again
I 'spect we never shall
But he'll remain in all our hearts
– a buddy friend and pal.

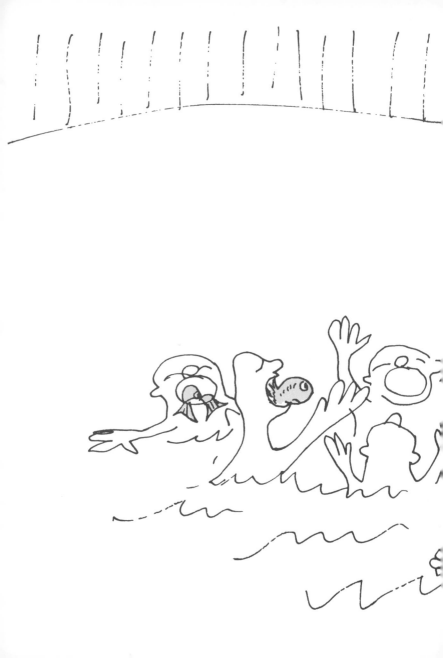

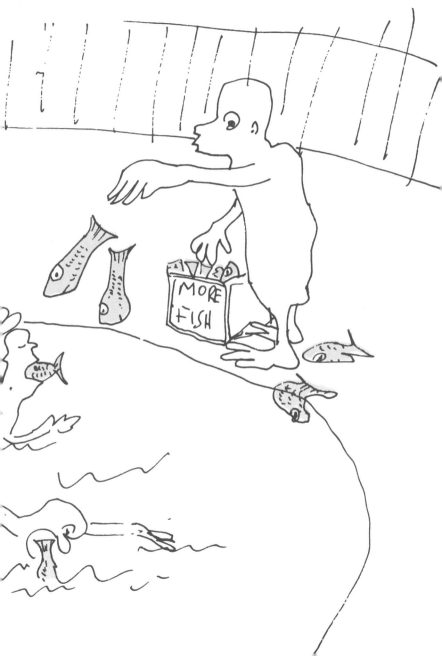

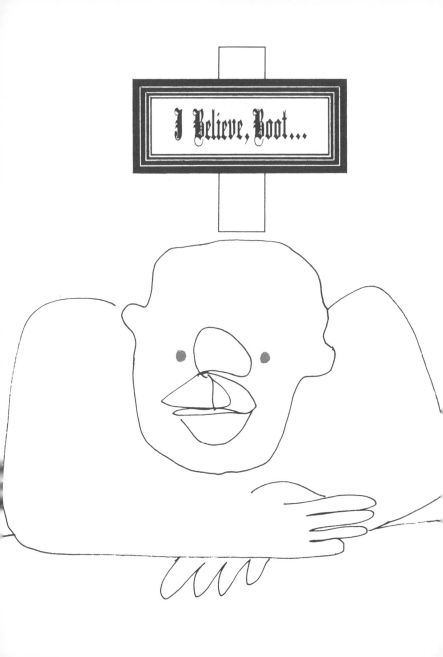

Aman came up to me the other day and said – 'Tell me
vicar – tell me the deafinition of sin?' – and you know, I
couldn't answer him! Which makes me think – do you ever
wonder (and what do we mean by the word wonder?) what
an ordinary man (and what – I ask myself do we mean by
an ordinary man?) who works in office or factory – goes
to church on Sunday (what exactly do we mean by
Sunday?) who is also a sinner (we are all sinners).
People are always coming up to me and asking – 'Why, if
Griff is so good and almighty – why does he bring such
misery into the world?' – and I can truthfully say St. Alf – ch
8 verse 5 – page 9. 'Griff walks in such mysterious ways
His woodwork to perform' (what do we mean by perform?)
Which leads me neatly, I feel, to our next guest for tonight –
A man whom is stickle trodding the pathway to our beloved
Griff – slowly but slowly I am here to help with the bridges he
must surely crooss. – 'Welcome to our studios tonight Mr
Wabooba (a foreigner)'

Mr W. 'Hellow you Rev boy.'

Rev.   Well! Mr Wobooba – may I call you Wog? What is
        the basic problem you are facing? (He smiles)

Mr W. 'You! white trash christian boy.' (He also smiles)

Rev.   Hmn! can you hallucinate? (He colours)

Mr W. 'I can.' (Colouring too)

Rev.   Well? (He smiles)

Mr W. 'Wot ah want to know man – is why almighty Griff
        continooally insists on straiking ma fellow blackpool
        inde fayse?'

Rev. A man travelling on a train – like you or I – to Scotland, had two or two bad eggs in his pocket – and you know – no one would sit by him.

Mr W. 'But ah dont see dat yo' christship. Ah mean, ah don't see de relevence.'

Rev. Well, Wabooba – let me put it this way. In Griff's eye, we are all a bunch of bananas – swaying in the breeze – waiting as it were, Wabooba – to be peeled by His great andunderstanding love – some of them fall on stonycroft – and some fall on the waistcoat.

Mr W. 'Well yo' worship, ah says dat if de Griff don't laike de peoples in de world starfing an' all dat c'n you tell me why dat de Pope have all dem rich robesan' jewelry an big house to live – when ma people could fit too tousand or mo' in dat Vatican Hall – and also de Arch bitter of Canterbubble – him too!'

Rev. Ai don't think that the Arch bishoff would like to live in the Vatican with that many people Mr Wabooba – besides he's C. of E.

Mr W. 'Ah don't mean dat you white trash christmas im⁄perialist!'

Rev. No one has ever called ME an imperialist before, Mr Wabooba. (He smiles)

Mr W. 'Well ah have.' (Smiling too)

Rev. You certainly have Mr Wabooba.

(He turns
other chin and leans forward slowly looking at Mr
Wabooba rather hard. Mr Wabooba leans forward
rather more quickly and they both kiss.)

Mr W. 'Ah forgive you in de name of Fatty Waller de great
savious of ma people.' (He smiles)

Rev. Ai too am capable of compassion dear Wabooba –
and in the name of the Fahter, Sock and Micky
Most, I forgive you sweet brother.
(With that they clasp each other in a brotherly way
as if forgetting they are still on camera.)

Rev. Have you ever been to Brighton dear Watooba?

Mr W. 'Ah jes' got back sweet christian friend non de worse
for wearing.' (They get up glassy eyed and linking arms
slowly walk out of the studio to the very left proving
that arbitration is one answer to de prodlem.)
FADE OUT ON SUITABLE CHRISTIAN
CAPTIONS

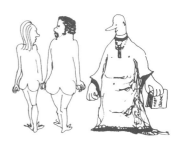

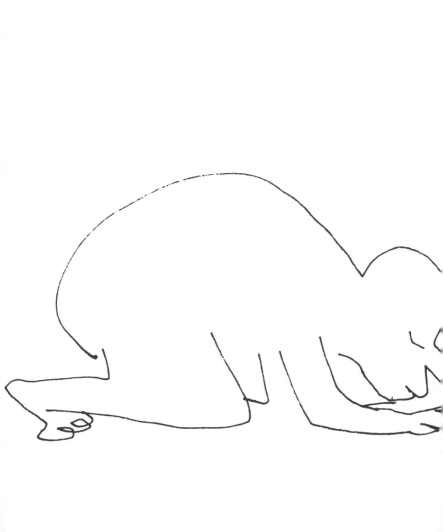

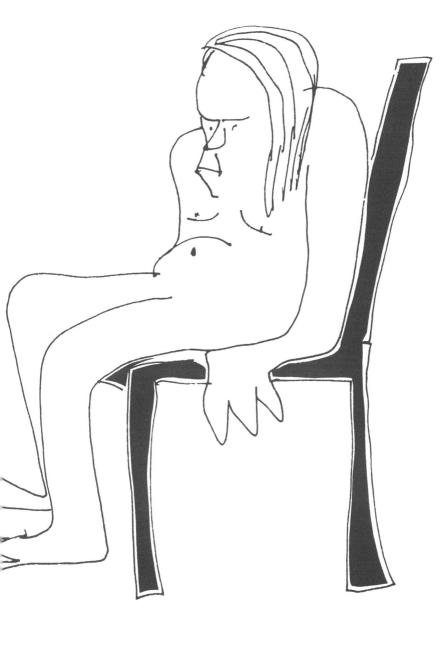

The End